Accuplacer® Skill Practice!

Accuplacer® Practice Test Questions

Published by

Complete TEST Preparation Inc.

Version 6.6 October 2015

We strongly recommend that students check with exam providers for up-to-date information regarding test content.

ISBN-13: 9781772450903

Published by
Complete Test Preparation Inc.
Victoria BC Canada
Visit us on the web at http://www.test-preparation.ca
Printed in the USA

About Complete Test Preparation Inc.

Complete Test Preparation Inc. has been publishing high quality study materials since 2005. Thousands of students visit our websites every year, and thousands of students, teachers and parents all over the world have purchased our teaching materials, curriculum, study guides and practice tests.

Complete Test Preparation Inc. is committed to providing students with the best study materials and practice tests available on the market. Members of our team combine years of teaching experience, with experienced writers and editors, all with advanced degrees.

Team Members for this publication

Editor: Brian Stocker MA
Contributor: Dr. C. Gregory
Contributor: Dr. G. A. Stocker DDS
Contributor: D. A. Stocker M. Ed.
Contributor: Elizabeta Petrovic MSc (Mathematics)

The Environment and Sustainability

Environmental consciousness is important for the continued growth of our company. In addition to eco-balancing each title, as a print on demand publisher, we only print units as orders come in, which greatly reduces excess printing and waste. This revolutionary printing technology also eliminates carbon emissions from trucks hauling boxes of books everywhere to warehouses. We also maintain a commitment to recycling any waste materials that may result from the printing process. We continue to review our manufacturing practices on an ongoing basis to ensure we are doing our part to protect and improve the environment.

Feedback

We welcome your feedback. Email us at feedback@test-preparation.ca with your comments and suggestions. We carefully review all suggestions and often incorporate reader suggestions into upcoming versions. As a Print on Demand Publisher, we update our products frequently.

 Find us on Facebook
www.facebook.com/CompleteTestPreparation

Contents

Getting Started

CONGRATULATIONS! By deciding to take the Accuplacer® Exam, you have taken the first step toward a great future! Of course, there is no point in taking this important examination unless you intend to do your very best to earn the highest grade you possibly can. That means getting yourself organized and discovering the best approaches, methods and strategies to master the material. Yes, that will require real effort and dedication on your part but if you are willing to focus your energy and devote the study time necessary, before you know it you will be on you will be opening that letter of acceptance to the school of your dreams!

We know that taking on a new endeavour can be a little scary, and it is easy to feel unsure of where to begin. That's where we come in. This study guide is designed to help you improve your test-taking skills, show you a few tricks of the

trade and increase both your competency and confidence.

The Accuplacer® Exam

The Accuplacer® exam is composed of four sections, reading, mathematics, sentence skills and writing. The reading section consists of reading comprehension questions. The mathematics section contains three sections, arithmetic, algebra and college level math. The sentence skills section contains questions on sentence structure and rewriting sentences. The writing section contains an essay question.

While we seek to make our guide as comprehensive as possible, note that like all exams, the Accuplacer® Exam might be adjusted at some future point. New material might be added, or content that is no longer relevant or applicable might be removed. It is always a good idea to give the materials you receive when you register to take the Accuplacer® a careful review.

The Accuplacer® Study Plan

Now that you have made the decision to take the Accuplacer®, it is time to get started. Before you do another thing, you will need to figure out a plan of attack. The very best study tip is to start early! The longer the time period you devote to regular study practice, the more likely you will be to retain the material and be able to access it quickly. If you thought that 1x20 is the same as 2x10, guess what? It really is not, when it comes to study time. Reviewing material for just an hour per day over the course of 20 days is far better than studying for two hours a day for only 10 days. The more often you revisit a particular piece of information, the better you will know it. Not only will your grasp and understanding be better, but your ability to reach into your brain and quickly and efficiently pull out the tidbit you need, will be greatly enhanced as well.

The great Chinese scholar and philosopher Confucius believed that true knowledge could be defined as knowing what you know and what you do not know. The first step in preparing for the Accuplacer® is to assess your strengths and weaknesses. You may already have an idea of what you know and what you do not know, but evaluating yourself using our Self- Assessment modules for each of the three areas, Math, Writing and Reading Comprehension, will clarify the details.

Making a Study Schedule

To make your study time most productive you will need to develop a study plan. The purpose of the plan is to organize all the bits of pieces of information in such a way that you will not feel overwhelmed. Rome was not built in a day, and learning everything you will need to know to pass the Accuplacer® is going to take time, too. Arranging the material you need to learn into manageable chunks is the best way to go. Each study session should make you feel as though you have succeeded in accomplishing your goal, and your goal is simply to learn what you planned to learn during that particular session. Try to organize the content in such a way that each study session builds on previous ones. That way, you will retain the information, be better able to access it, and review the previous bits and pieces at the same time.

Self-assessment

The Best Study Tip! The very best study tip is to start early! The longer you study regularly, the more you will retain and 'learn' the material. Studying for 1 hour per day for 20 days is far better than studying for 2 hours for 10 days.

What don't you know?

The first step is to assess your strengths and weaknesses. You may already have an idea of where your weaknesses are, or you can take our Self-assessment modules for each of the areas, Math, English, Science and Reading Comprehension.

Exam Component	Rate 1 to 5
Reading Comprehension	
Making Inferences	
Main idea	
Arithmetic	
Decimals Percent and Fractions	
Problem solving (Word Problems)	
Basic Algebra	

Simple Geometry	
Problem Solving	
Essay Writing	
Sentence Skills	
Sentence Correction	
Sentence Shift	
Basic English Grammar and Usage	
Algebra	
Exponents	
Linear Equations	
Quadratics	
Polynomials	
College Level	
Coordinate Geometry	
Trigonometry	
Polynomials	
Logarithms	
Sequences	

Making a Study Schedule

The key to making a study plan is to divide the material you need to learn into manageable size and learn it, while at the same time reviewing the material that you already know.

Using the table above, any scores of three or below, you need to spend time learning, going over and practicing this subject area. A score of four means you need to review the material, but you don't have to spend time re-learning. A score of five and you are OK with just an occasional review before the exam.

A score of zero or one means you really do need to work on this and you should allocate the most time and give it the highest priority. Some students prefer a 5-day plan and others a 10-day plan. It also depends on how much time you have until the exam.

Here is an example of a 5-day plan based on an example from the table above:

Main Idea: 1   Study 1 hour everyday – review on last day
Fractions: 3   Study 1 hour for 2 days then ½ hour and then review
Algebra: 4   Review every second day
Grammar & Usage: 2 Study 1 hour on the first day – then ½ hour everyday
Reading Comprehension: 5   Review for ½ hour every other day
Geometry: 5 Review for ½ hour every other day

Using this example, geometry and reading comprehension are good and only need occasional review. Algebra is good and needs 'some' review. Fractions need a bit of work, grammar and usage needs a lot of work and Main Idea is very weak and need the majority of time. Based on this, here is a sample study plan:

Day	Subject	Time
Monday		
Study	Main Idea	1 hour
Study	Grammar & Usage	1 hour
	½ hour break	
Study	Fractions	1 hour
Review	Algebra	½ hour
Tuesday		
Study	Main Idea	1 hour
Study	Grammar & Usage	½ hour
	½ hour break	
Study	Fractions	½ hour
Review	Algebra	½ hour

Review	Geometry	½ hour
Wednesday		
Study	Main Idea	1 hour
Study	Grammar & Usage	½ hour
	½ hour break	
Study	Fractions	½ hour
Review	Geometry	½ hour
Thursday		
Study	Main Idea	½ hour
Study	Grammar & Usage	½ hour
Review	Fractions	½ hour
	½ hour break	
Review	Geometry	½ hour
Review	Algebra	½ hour
Friday		
Review	Main Idea	½ hour
Review	Grammar & Usage	½ hour
Review	Fractions	½ hour
	½ hour break	
Review	Algebra	½ hour
Review	Grammar & Usage	½ hour

Using this example, adapt the study plan to your own schedule. This schedule assumes 2 ½ - 3 hours available to study everyday for a 5 day period.

First, write out what you need to study and how much. Next figure out how many days you have before the test. Note, do NOT study on the last day before the test. On the last day before the test, you won't learn anything and will probably only confuse yourself.

Make a table with the days before the test and the number of hours you have available to study each day. We suggest working with 1 hour and ½ hour time slots.

Start filling in the blanks, with the subjects you need to study the most getting the most time and the most regular time slots (i.e. everyday) and the subjects that you know getting the least time (e.g. ½ hour every other day, or every 3rd day).

Tips for making a schedule

Once you make a schedule, stick with it! Make your study sessions reasonable. If you make a study schedule and don't stick with it, you set yourself up for failure. Instead, schedule study sessions that are a bit shorter and set yourself up for success! Make sure your study sessions are do-able. Studying is hard work but after you pass, you can party and take a break!

Schedule breaks. Breaks are just as important as study time. Work out a rotation of studying and breaks that works for you.

Build up study time. If you find it hard to sit still and study for 1 hour straight through, build up to it. Start with 20 minutes, and then take a break. Once you get used to 20-minute study sessions, increase the time to 30 minutes. Gradually work you way up to 1 hour.

40 minutes to 1 hour are optimal. Studying for longer than this is tiring and not productive. Studying for shorter isn't long enough to be productive.

Studying Math. Studying Math is different from studying other subjects because you use a different part of your brain. The best way to study math is to practice everyday. This will train your mind to think in a mathematical way. If you miss a day or days, the mathematical mind-set is gone and you have to start all over again to build it up.

Study and practice math everyday for at least 5 days before the exam.

Practice Test Questions Set 1

The questions below are not the same as you will find on the Accuplacer® - that would be too easy! And nobody knows what the questions will be and they change all the time. Below are general questions that cover the same subject areas as the Accuplacer®. So, while the format and exact wording of the questions may differ slightly, and change from year to year, if you can answer the questions below, you will have no problem with the Accuplacer®.

For the best results, take these practice test questions as if it were the real exam. Set aside time when you will not be disturbed, and a location that is quiet and free of distractions. Read the instructions carefully, read each question carefully, and answer to the best of your ability.
Use the bubble answer sheets provided. When you have completed the practice questions, check your answer against the Answer Key and read the explanation provided.

Do not attempt more than one set of practice test questions in one day. After completing the first practice test, wait two or three days before attempting the second set of questions.

Reading Answer Sheet

1. Ⓐ Ⓑ Ⓒ Ⓓ   11. Ⓐ Ⓑ Ⓒ Ⓓ   21. Ⓐ Ⓑ Ⓒ Ⓓ

2. Ⓐ Ⓑ Ⓒ Ⓓ   12. Ⓐ Ⓑ Ⓒ Ⓓ   22. Ⓐ Ⓑ Ⓒ Ⓓ

3. Ⓐ Ⓑ Ⓒ Ⓓ   13. Ⓐ Ⓑ Ⓒ Ⓓ   23. Ⓐ Ⓑ Ⓒ Ⓓ

4. Ⓐ Ⓑ Ⓒ Ⓓ   14. Ⓐ Ⓑ Ⓒ Ⓓ   24. Ⓐ Ⓑ Ⓒ Ⓓ

5. Ⓐ Ⓑ Ⓒ Ⓓ   15. Ⓐ Ⓑ Ⓒ Ⓓ   25. Ⓐ Ⓑ Ⓒ Ⓓ

6. Ⓐ Ⓑ Ⓒ Ⓓ   16. Ⓐ Ⓑ Ⓒ Ⓓ   26. Ⓐ Ⓑ Ⓒ Ⓓ

7. Ⓐ Ⓑ Ⓒ Ⓓ   17. Ⓐ Ⓑ Ⓒ Ⓓ   27. Ⓐ Ⓑ Ⓒ Ⓓ

8. Ⓐ Ⓑ Ⓒ Ⓓ   18. Ⓐ Ⓑ Ⓒ Ⓓ   28. Ⓐ Ⓑ Ⓒ Ⓓ

9. Ⓐ Ⓑ Ⓒ Ⓓ   19. Ⓐ Ⓑ Ⓒ Ⓓ   29. Ⓐ Ⓑ Ⓒ Ⓓ

10. Ⓐ Ⓑ Ⓒ Ⓓ   20. Ⓐ Ⓑ Ⓒ Ⓓ   30. Ⓐ Ⓑ Ⓒ Ⓓ

Mathematics Answer Sheet
(Arithmetic, Algebra and College Level Math)

1. Ⓐ Ⓑ Ⓒ Ⓓ   21. Ⓐ Ⓑ Ⓒ Ⓓ   41. Ⓐ Ⓑ Ⓒ Ⓓ

2. Ⓐ Ⓑ Ⓒ Ⓓ   22. Ⓐ Ⓑ Ⓒ Ⓓ   42. Ⓐ Ⓑ Ⓒ Ⓓ

3. Ⓐ Ⓑ Ⓒ Ⓓ   23. Ⓐ Ⓑ Ⓒ Ⓓ   43. Ⓐ Ⓑ Ⓒ Ⓓ

4. Ⓐ Ⓑ Ⓒ Ⓓ   24. Ⓐ Ⓑ Ⓒ Ⓓ   44. Ⓐ Ⓑ Ⓒ Ⓓ

5. Ⓐ Ⓑ Ⓒ Ⓓ   25. Ⓐ Ⓑ Ⓒ Ⓓ   45. Ⓐ Ⓑ Ⓒ Ⓓ

6. Ⓐ Ⓑ Ⓒ Ⓓ   26. Ⓐ Ⓑ Ⓒ Ⓓ   46. Ⓐ Ⓑ Ⓒ Ⓓ

7. Ⓐ Ⓑ Ⓒ Ⓓ   27. Ⓐ Ⓑ Ⓒ Ⓓ   47. Ⓐ Ⓑ Ⓒ Ⓓ

8. Ⓐ Ⓑ Ⓒ Ⓓ   28. Ⓐ Ⓑ Ⓒ Ⓓ   48. Ⓐ Ⓑ Ⓒ Ⓓ

9. Ⓐ Ⓑ Ⓒ Ⓓ   29. Ⓐ Ⓑ Ⓒ Ⓓ   49. Ⓐ Ⓑ Ⓒ Ⓓ

10. Ⓐ Ⓑ Ⓒ Ⓓ   30. Ⓐ Ⓑ Ⓒ Ⓓ   50. Ⓐ Ⓑ Ⓒ Ⓓ

11. Ⓐ Ⓑ Ⓒ Ⓓ   31. Ⓐ Ⓑ Ⓒ Ⓓ   51. Ⓐ Ⓑ Ⓒ Ⓓ

12. Ⓐ Ⓑ Ⓒ Ⓓ   32. Ⓐ Ⓑ Ⓒ Ⓓ   52. Ⓐ Ⓑ Ⓒ Ⓓ

13. Ⓐ Ⓑ Ⓒ Ⓓ   33. Ⓐ Ⓑ Ⓒ Ⓓ   53. Ⓐ Ⓑ Ⓒ Ⓓ

14. Ⓐ Ⓑ Ⓒ Ⓓ   34. Ⓐ Ⓑ Ⓒ Ⓓ   54. Ⓐ Ⓑ Ⓒ Ⓓ

15. Ⓐ Ⓑ Ⓒ Ⓓ   35. Ⓐ Ⓑ Ⓒ Ⓓ   55. Ⓐ Ⓑ Ⓒ Ⓓ

16. Ⓐ Ⓑ Ⓒ Ⓓ   36. Ⓐ Ⓑ Ⓒ Ⓓ   56. Ⓐ Ⓑ Ⓒ Ⓓ

17. Ⓐ Ⓑ Ⓒ Ⓓ   37. Ⓐ Ⓑ Ⓒ Ⓓ   57. Ⓐ Ⓑ Ⓒ Ⓓ

18. Ⓐ Ⓑ Ⓒ Ⓓ   38. Ⓐ Ⓑ Ⓒ Ⓓ   58. Ⓐ Ⓑ Ⓒ Ⓓ

19. Ⓐ Ⓑ Ⓒ Ⓓ   39. Ⓐ Ⓑ Ⓒ Ⓓ   59. Ⓐ Ⓑ Ⓒ Ⓓ

20. Ⓐ Ⓑ Ⓒ Ⓓ   40. Ⓐ Ⓑ Ⓒ Ⓓ   60. Ⓐ Ⓑ Ⓒ Ⓓ

Sentence Skills Answer Sheet

1. Ⓐ Ⓑ Ⓒ Ⓓ   11. Ⓐ Ⓑ Ⓒ Ⓓ

2. Ⓐ Ⓑ Ⓒ Ⓓ   12. Ⓐ Ⓑ Ⓒ Ⓓ

3. Ⓐ Ⓑ Ⓒ Ⓓ   13. Ⓐ Ⓑ Ⓒ Ⓓ

4. Ⓐ Ⓑ Ⓒ Ⓓ   14. Ⓐ Ⓑ Ⓒ Ⓓ

5. Ⓐ Ⓑ Ⓒ Ⓓ   15. Ⓐ Ⓑ Ⓒ Ⓓ

6. Ⓐ Ⓑ Ⓒ Ⓓ   16. Ⓐ Ⓑ Ⓒ Ⓓ

7. Ⓐ Ⓑ Ⓒ Ⓓ   17. Ⓐ Ⓑ Ⓒ Ⓓ

8. Ⓐ Ⓑ Ⓒ Ⓓ   18. Ⓐ Ⓑ Ⓒ Ⓓ

9. Ⓐ Ⓑ Ⓒ Ⓓ   19. Ⓐ Ⓑ Ⓒ Ⓓ

10. Ⓐ Ⓑ Ⓒ Ⓓ   20. Ⓐ Ⓑ Ⓒ Ⓓ

Part 1 - Reading

Questions 1 – 4 refer to the following passage.

The Life of Helen Keller

Many people have heard of Helen Keller. She is famous because she was unable to see or hear, but learned to speak and read and went onto attend college and earn a degree. Her life is a very interesting story, one that she developed into an autobiography, which was then adapted into both a stage play and a movie. How did Helen Keller overcome her disabilities to become a famous woman? Read onto find out. Helen Keller was not born blind and deaf. When she was a small baby, she had a very high fever for several days. As a result of her sudden illness, baby Helen lost her eyesight and her hearing. Because she was so young when she went deaf and blind, Helen Keller never had any recollection of being able to see or hear. Since she could not hear, she could not learn to talk. Since she could not see, it was difficult for her to move around. For the first six years of her life, her world was very still and dark.

Imagine what Helen's childhood must have been like. She could not hear her mother's voice. She could not see the beauty of her parent's farm. She could not recognize who was giving her a hug, or a bath or even where her bedroom was each night. More sad, she could not communicate with her parents in any way. She could not express her feelings or tell them the things she wanted. It must have been a very sad childhood.

When Helen was six years old, her parents hired her a teacher named Anne Sullivan. Anne was a young woman who was almost blind. However, she could hear and she could read Braille, so she was a perfect teacher for young Helen. At first, Anne had a very hard time teaching Helen anything. She described her first impression of Helen as a "wild thing, not a child." Helen did not like Anne at first either. She bit and hit Anne when Anne tried to teach her. However, the two of them eventually came to have a great deal of love and respect.

Anne taught Helen to hear by putting her hands on people's throats. She could feel the sounds that people made. In time, Helen learned to feel what people said. Next, Anne taught Helen to read Braille, which is a way that books are written for the blind. Finally, Anne taught Helen to talk. Although Helen did learn to talk, it was hard for anyone but Anne to understand her.

As Helen grew older, more and more people were amazed by her story. She went to college and wrote books about her life. She gave talks to the public, with Anne at her side, translating her words. Today, both Anne Sullivan and Helen Keller are famous women who are respected for their lives' work.

1. Helen Keller could not see and hear and so, what was her biggest problem in childhood?

    a. Inability to communicate

    b. Inability to walk

    c. Inability to play

    d. Inability to eat

2. Helen learned to hear by feeling the vibrations people made when they spoke. What were these vibrations were felt through?

    a. Mouth

    b. Throat

    c. Ears

    d. Lips

3. From the passage, we can infer that Anne Sullivan was a patient teacher. We can infer this because

a. Helen hit and bit her and Anne still remained her teacher.

b. Anne taught Helen to read only.

c. Anne was hard of hearing too.

d. Anne wanted to be a teacher.

4. Helen Keller learned to speak but Anne translated her words when she spoke in public. The reason Helen needed a translator was because

a. Helen spoke another language.

b. Helen's words were hard for people to understand.

c. Helen spoke very quietly.

d. Helen did not speak but only used sign language.

Questions 5 – 7 refer to the following passage.

Thunderstorms

The first stage of a thunderstorm is the cumulus stage, or developing stage. In this stage, masses of moisture are lifted upwards into the atmosphere. The trigger for this lift can be insulation heating the ground producing thermals, areas where two winds converge, forcing air upwards, or, where winds blow over terrain of increasing elevation. Moisture in the air rapidly cools into liquid drops of water, which appears as cumulus clouds.

As the water vapor condenses into liquid, latent heat is released which warms the air, causing it to become less dense than the surrounding dry air. The warm air rises in an updraft through the process of convection (hence the term convective precipitation). This creates a low-pressure zone beneath the forming thunderstorm. In a typical thunderstorm, about 5×10^8 kg of water vapor is lifted, and the quantity of energy released when this condenses is about equal to the energy used by a city of 100,000 in a month. [1]

5. The cumulus stage of a thunderstorm is the

    a. The last stage of the storm.

    b. The middle stage of the storm formation.

    c. The beginning of the thunderstorm.

    d. The period after the thunderstorm has ended.

6. One of the ways the air is warmed is

    a. Air moving downwards, which creates a high-pressure zone.

    b. Air cooling and becoming less dense, causing it to rise.

    c. Moisture moving downward toward the earth.

    d. Heat created by water vapor condensing into liquid.

7. Identify the correct sequence of events.

    a. Warm air rises, water droplets condense, creating more heat, and the air rises farther.

    b. Warm air rises and cools, water droplets condense, causing low pressure.

    c. Warm air rises and collects water vapor, the water vapor condenses as the air rises, which creates heat, and causes the air to rise farther.

    d. None of the above.

Questions 8 – 10 refer to the following passage.

What Is Mardi Gras?

Mardi Gras is fast becoming one of the South's most famous and most celebrated holidays. The word Mardi Gras comes from the French and the literal translation is "Fat Tuesday."

The holiday has also been called Shrove Tuesday, due to its associations with Lent. The purpose of Mardi Gras is to celebrate and enjoy before the Lenten season of fasting and repentance begins.

What originated by the French Explorers in New Orleans, Louisiana in the 17th century is now celebrated all over the world. Panama, Italy, Belgium and Brazil all host large scale Mardi Gras celebrations, and many smaller cities and towns celebrate this fun loving Tuesday as well. Usually held in February or early March, Mardi Gras is a day of extravagance, a day for people to eat, drink and be merry, to wear costumes, masks and to dance to jazz music.
The French explorers on the Mississippi River would be in shock today if they saw the opulence of the parades and floats that grace the New Orleans streets during Mardi Gras these days. Parades in New Orleans are divided by organizations. These are more commonly known as Krewes.

Being a member of a Krewe is quite a task because Krewes are responsible for overseeing the parades. Each Krewe's parade is ruled by a Mardi Gras "King and Queen." The role of the King and Queen is to "bestow" gifts on their adoring fans as the floats ride along the street. They throw doubloons, which is fake money and usually colored green, purple and gold, which are the colors of Mardi Gras. Beads in those color shades are also thrown and cups are thrown as well. Beads are by far the most popular souvenir of any Mardi Gras parade, with each spectator attempting to gather as many as possible.

8. The purpose of Mardi Gras is to

    a. Repent for a month.

    b. Celebrate in extravagant ways.

    c. Be a member of a Krewe.

    d. Explore the Mississippi.

9. From reading the passage we can infer that "Kings and Queens"

    a. Have to be members of a Krewe.

    b. Have to be French.

    c. Have to know how to speak French.

    d. Have to give away their own money.

10. Which group of people first began to hold Mardi Gras celebrations?

    a. Settlers from Italy

    b. Members of Krewes

    c. French explorers

    d. Belgium explorers

Questions 11 – 13 refer to the following passage.

Clouds

A cloud is a visible mass of droplets or frozen crystals floating in the atmosphere above the surface of the Earth or other planetary bodies. Another type of cloud is a mass of material in space, attracted by gravity, called interstellar clouds and nebulae. The branch of meteorology which studies clouds is called nephrology. When we are speaking of Earth clouds, water vapor is usually the condensing substance, which forms small droplets or ice crystal. These crystals are typically 0.01 mm in diameter. Dense, deep clouds reflect most light, so they appear white, at least from the top. Cloud droplets scatter light very efficiently, so the farther into a cloud light travels, the weaker it gets. This accounts for the gray or dark appearance at the base of large clouds. Thin clouds may appear to have acquired the color of their environment or background. [2]

11. What are clouds made of?

a. Water droplets

b. Ice crystals

c. Ice crystals and water droplets

d. Clouds on Earth are made of ice crystals and water droplets

12. The main idea of this passage is

a. Condensation occurs in clouds, having an intense effect on the weather on the surface of the earth.

b. Atmospheric gases are responsible for the gray color of clouds just before a severe storm happens.

c. A cloud is a visible mass of droplets or frozen crystals floating in the atmosphere above the surface of the Earth or other planetary body.

d. Clouds reflect light in varying amounts and degrees, depending on the size and concentration of the water droplets.

13. Why are clouds white on top and grey on the bottom?

a. Because water droplets inside the cloud do not reflect light, it appears white, and the farther into the cloud the light travels, the less light is reflected making the bottom appear dark.

b. Because water droplets outside the cloud reflect light, it appears dark, and the farther into the cloud the light travels, the more light is reflected making the bottom appear white.

c. Because water droplets inside the cloud reflects light, making it appear white, and the farther into the cloud the light travels, the more light is reflected making the bottom appear dark.

d. None of the above.

Questions 14 - 17 refer to the following passage.

Keeping Tropical Fish

Keeping tropical fish at home or in your office used to be
very popular. Today, interest has declined, but it remains
as rewarding and relaxing a hobby as ever. Ask any tropical
fish hobbyist, and you will hear how soothing and relaxing
watching colorful fish live their lives in the aquarium. If you
are considering keeping tropical fish as pets, here is a list of
the basic equipment you will need.

A filter is essential for keeping your aquarium clean and
your fish alive and healthy. There are different types and
sizes of filters and the right size for you depends on the size
of the aquarium and the level of stocking. Generally, you
need a filter with a 3 to 5 times turn over rate per hour. This
means that the water in the tank should go through the filter about 3 to 5 times per hour.

Most tropical fish do well in water temperatures ranging
between 24ºC and 26ºC, though each has its own ideal water
temperature. A heater with a thermostat is necessary to
regulate the water temperature. Some heaters are submers-
ible and others are not, so check carefully before you buy.
Lights are also necessary, and come in a large variety of
types, strengths and sizes. A light source is necessary for
plants in the tank to photosynthesize and give the tank a
more attractive appearance. Even if you plan to use plastic
plants, the fish still require light, although here you can use
a lower strength light source.

 A hood is necessary to keep dust, dirt and unwanted materials out of the tank. Sometimes the hood can also help
prevent evaporation. Another requirement is aquarium
gravel. This will improve the aesthetics of the aquarium and
is necessary if you plan to have real plants.

14. What is the general tone of this article?

a. Formal

b. Informal

c. Technical

d. Opinion

15. Which of the following cannot be inferred?

a. Gravel is good for aquarium plants.

b. Fewer people have aquariums in their office than at home.

c. The larger the tank, the larger the filter required.

d. None of the above.

16. What evidence does the author provide to support their claim that aquarium lights are necessary?

a. Plants require light.

b. Fish and plants require light.

c. The author does not provide evidence for this statement.

d. Aquarium lights make the aquarium more attractive.

17. Which of the following is an opinion?

a. Filter with a 3 to 5 times turn over rate per hour are required.

b. Aquarium gravel improves the aesthetics of the aquarium.

c. An aquarium hood keeps dust, dirt and unwanted materials out of the tank.

d. Each type of tropical fish has its own ideal water temperature.

Questions 18 - 20 refer to the following passage.

Ways Characters Communicate in Theater

Playwrights give their characters voices in a way that gives depth and added meaning to what happens on stage during their play. There are different types of speech in scripts that allow characters to talk with themselves, with other characters, and even with the audience.

It is very unique to theater that characters may talk "to themselves." When characters do this, the speech they give is called a soliloquy. Soliloquies are usually poetic, introspective, moving, and can tell audience members about the feelings, motivations, or suspicions of an individual character without that character having to reveal them to other characters on stage. "To be or not to be" is a famous soliloquy given by Hamlet as he considers difficult but important themes, such as life and death.

The most common type of communication in plays is when one character is speaking to another or a group of other characters. This is generally called dialogue, but can also be called monologue if one character speaks without being interrupted for a long time. It is not necessarily the most important type of communication, but it is the most common because the plot of the play cannot really progress without it.

Lastly, and most unique to theater (although it has been used somewhat in film) is when a character speaks directly to the audience. This is called an aside, and scripts usually specifically direct actors to do this. Asides are usually comical, an inside joke between the character and the audience, and very short. The actor will usually face the audience when delivering them, even if it's for a moment, so the audience can recognize this move as an aside.

All three of these types of communication are important to the art of theater, and have been perfected by famous playwrights like Shakespeare. Understanding these types of communication can help an audience member grasp what is artful about the script and action of a play.

18. According to the passage, characters in plays communicate to

a. move the plot forward

b. show the private thoughts and feelings of one character

c. make the audience laugh

d. add beauty and artistry to the play

19. When Hamlet delivers "To be or not to be," he can most likely be described as

a. solitary

b. thoughtful

c. dramatic

d. hopeless

20. The author uses parentheses to punctuate "although it has been used somewhat in film"

a. to show that films are less important

b. instead of using commas so that the sentence is not interrupted

c. because parenthesis help separate details that are not as important

d. to show that films are not as artistic

Instructions: For each of the questions below, you are given 2 sentences, followed by a question about the relationship between the 2 sentences. Choose the best answer that describes the relationship.

21. An example of a cold-blooded animal that hibernates underground during the winter is the snake.

Snakes, such as garter snakes and western rattlesnakes, hibernate underground in large groups during the winter.

    a. The second sentence reinforces the first.

    b. The second sentence analyzes a statement made in the first.

    c. The second sentence proposes a solution.

    d. The second sentence draws a conclusion.

22. The dog barked and ran.

The dog barked and ran after the postman who was delivering mail.

    a. The second sentence analyzes a statement made in the first.

    b. The second sentence reinforces the first.

    c. The second sentence expands on the first.

    d. The second sentence proposes a solution.

24. Aphids, pest commonly found on roses, are destroying my rose bushes.

If I spray my rose bushes with insecticidal soap, I will kill the aphids.

    a. The second sentence draws a conclusion.

    b. The second sentence reinforces the first.

    c. The second sentence analyzes a statement made in the first.

    d. The second sentence proposes a solution.

25. Ms. Apple received and reviewed her students', who all scored on the 99th percentile on the standardized test.

She discovered that most of her students performed at the highest level of achievement; thus, they mastered the material and skills taught.

a. The second sentence reinforces the first.

b. The second sentence proposes a solution.

c. The second sentence analyzes a statement made in the first.

d. The second sentence expands on the first.

26. Human activities have contributed to global warming.

Due to global warming, hurricanes, tornadoes and other storms will become stronger and more frequent.

a. The second sentence contrasts the first.

b. The second sentence restates an idea in the first sentence.

c. The second sentence states an effect.

d. The second sentence gives an example.

27. Jungles and rainforests are both associated with tropical climates.

Vegetation in jungles are tangled and impenetrable (hard to walk through without cutting your way through); however, vegetation in the rainforest is sparse.

a. The second sentence restates an idea in the first sentence.

b. The second sentence states an effect.

c. The second sentence gives an example.

d. The second sentence contrasts the first.

28. Rosaline's friend invited her to the Civil Rights Photography Exhibit at the local museum.

Rosaline did not know as much as she wanted to about the African-American Civil Rights Movement, so she went to the library and checked out books related to the African-American Civil Rights Movement.

    a. They repeat the same idea.

    b. They provide a problem and solution.

    c. They contradict each other.

    d. They reinforce each other.

29. Parrots and macaws are beautiful, colorful birds.

There are over 370 species of parrots, but there are only 18 species of macaws.

    a. They establish a contrast.

    b. They provide a problem and solution.

    c. They contradict each other.

    d. They reinforce each other.

30. Paris is often referred to as the "City of Lights."

Paris is called the "City of Lights" because there are over 296 illuminated sites and buildings in Paris, and most importantly, Paris was the birthplace of the Age of Enlightenment.

    a. They establish a contrast.

    b. They reinforce each other.

    c. They provide a problem and solution.

    d. They contradict each other.

Arithmetic

1. Brad has agreed to buy everyone a Coke. Each drink costs $1.89, and there are 5 friends. Estimate Brad's cost.

　　a. $7

　　b. $8

　　c. $10

　　d. $12

2. c = 4, n = 5 and x = 3. then 2cnx/2n =?

　　a. 12

　　b. 50

　　c. 8

　　d. 21

3. What fraction of $1500 is $75?

　　a. 1/14

　　b. 3/5

　　c. 7/10

　　d. 1/20

4. Estimate 16 x 230.

　　a. 31,000

　　b. 301,000

　　c. 3,100

　　d. 3,000,000

5. Below is the attendance for a class of 45.

Day	Number of Absent Students
Monday	5
Tuesday	9
Wednesday	4
Thursday	10
Friday	6

What is the average attendance for the week?

    a. 88%

    b. 85%

    c. 81%

    d. 77%

6. John purchased a jacket at a 7% discount. He had a membership which gave him an additional 2% discount on the discounted price. If he paid $425, what is the retail price of the jacket?

    a. $460

    b. $466

    c. $466

    d. $472

7. Estimate 215 x 65.

    a. 1,350

    b. 13,500

    c. 103,500

    d. 3,500

8. 10 x 2 – (7 + 9)

    a. 21

    b. 16

    c. 4

    d. 13

9. 40% of a number is equal to 90. What is the half of the number?

    a. 18

    b. 112.5

    c. 225

    d. 120

10. 1/4 + 3/10 =

    a. 9/10

    b. 11/20

    c. 7/15

    d. 3/40

11. A map uses a scale of 1:2,000   How much distance on the ground is 5.2 inches on the map if the scale is in inches?

    a. 100,400

    b. 10,500

    c. 10,400

    d. 1,400

12. A shop sells a piece of industrial equipment for $545. If 15% of the cost was added to the price as value added tax, what is the actual cost of the equipment?

  a. $490.40

  b. $473.91

  c. $505.00

  d. $503.15

13. What is 0.27 + 0.33 expressed as a fraction?

  a. 3/6

  b. 4/7

  c. 3/5

  d. 2/7

14. 5 men have to share a load weighing 10 kg 550 g equally among themselves. How much will each man carry?

  a. 900 g

  b. 1.5 kg

  c. 3 kg

  d. 2 kg 110 g

15. 1/4 + 11/16

  a. 9/16

  b. 1 1/16

  c. 11/16

  d. 15/16

16. **A square lawn has an area of 62,500 square meters. What is the cost of building fence around it at a rate of $5.5 per meter?**

    a. $4,000

    b. $5,500

    c. $4,500

    d. $5,000

17. A mother is 7 times older than her child. In 25 years, her age will be double that of her child. How old is the mother now?

    a. 35

    b. 33

    c. 30

    d. 25

18. Convert 0.28 to a fraction.

    a. 7/25

    b. 3.25

    c. 8/25

    d. 5/28

19. If a discount of 20% is given for a desk and Mark saves $45, how much did he pay for the desk?

    a. $225

    b. $160

    c. $180

    d. $210

20. In a grade 8 exam, students are asked to divide a number by 3/2, but a student mistakenly multiplied the number by 3/2 and the answer is 5 more than the required one. What was the number?

    a. 4

    b. 5

    c. 6

    d. 8

Algebra

21. Divide 243 by 3^3

    a. 243

    b. 11

    c. 9

    d. 27

22. Solve the following equation $4(y + 6) = 3y + 30$

    a. $y = 20$

    b. $y = 6$

    c. $y = 30/7$

    d. $y = 30$

23. Divide $x^2 - y^2$ by $x - y$.

    a. $x - y$

    b. $x + y$

    c. xy

    d. $y - x$

24. Solve for x if, 10^2 x $100^2 = 1000^x$

    a. x = 2

    b. x = 3

    c. x = -2

    d. x = 0

25. Given polynomials A = $-2x^4 + x^2 - 3x$, B = $x^4 - x^3 + 5$ and C = $x^4 + 2x^3 + 4x + 5$, find A + B - C.

    a. $x^3 + x^2 + x + 10$

    b. $-3x^3 + x^2 - 7x + 10$

    c. $-2x^4 - 3x^3 + x^2 - 7x$

    d. $-3x^4 + x^3 + 2 - 7x$

26. Solve the inequality: $(x - 6)^2 \geq x^2 + 12$

    a. $[2, + \infty)$

    b. $(2, + \infty)$

    c. $(-\infty, 2]$

    d. $(12, + \infty)$

27. $7^5 - 3^5$ =

    a. 15,000

    b. 16,564

    c. 15,800

    d. 15,007

28. Divide $x^3 - 3x^2 + 3x - 1$ by x - 1.

    a. $x^2 - 1$

    b. $x^2 + 1$

    c. $x^2 - 2x + 1$

    d. $x^2 + 2x + 1$

29. Express 9 x 9 x 9 in exponential form and standard form.

    a. $9^3 = 719$

    b. $9^3 = 629$

    c. $9^3 = 729$

    d. $10^3 = 729$

30. Using the factoring method, solve the quadratic equation: $x^2 - 5x - 6 = 0$

    a. -6 and 1

    b. -1 and 6

    c. 1 and 6

    d. -6 and -1

31. Divide 0.524 by 10^3

    a. 0.0524

    b. 0.000524

    c. 0.00524

    d. 524

32. Factor the polynomial $x^3y^3 - x^2y^8$.

    a. $x^2y^3(x - y^5)$

    b. $x^3y^3(1 - y^5)$

    c. $x^2y^2(x - y^6)$

    d. $xy^3(x - y^5)$

33. Find the solution for the following linear equation: $5x/2 = (3x + 24)/6$.

    a. -1

    b. 0

    c. 1

    d. 2

34. $3^2 \times 3^5$

    a. 3^{17}

    b. 3^5

    c. 4^8

    d. 3^7

35. Solve the system, if 'a' is some real number:

ax + y = 1
x + ay = 1

    a. (1,a)

    b. (1/a + 1, 1)

    c. (1/(a + 1), 1/(a + 1))

    d. (a, 1/a + 1)

36. Solve $3^5 \div 3^8$

    a. 3^3

    b. 3^5

    c. 3^6

    d. 3^4

37. Solve the linear equation: 3(x + 2) - 2(1 - x) = 4x + 5

    a. -1

    b. 0

    c. 1

    d. 2

38. Simplify the following expression: $3x^a + 6a^x - x^a +$ $(-5a^x) - 2x^a$

    a. $a^x + x^a$

    b. $a^x - x^a$

    c. a^x

    d. x^a

39. Add polynomials $-3x^2 + 2x + 6$ and $-x^2 - x - 1$.

    a. $-2x^2 + x + 5$

    b. $-4x^2 + x + 5$

    c. $-2x^2 + 3x + 5$

    d. $-4x^2 + 3x + 5$

40. 10^4 is not equal to which of the following?

    a. 100,000

    b. 10 x 10 x 10 x 10

    c. 10^2 x 10^2

    d. 10,000

College Level

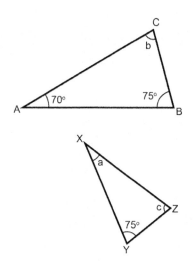

41. What are the respective values of a, b & c if both triangles are similar?

    a. 70°, 70°, 35°

    b. 70°, 35°, 70°

    c. 35°, 35°, 35°

    d. 70°, 35°, 35°

42. For what x is the following equation correct:

$$\log_x 125 = 3$$

    a. 1

    b. 2

    c. 3

    d. 5

43. What is the value of the expression $(1 - 4\sin^2(\pi/6))/(1 + 4\cos^2(\pi/3))$?

    a. -2

    b. -1

    c. 0

    d. 1/2

44. Calculate $(\sin^2 30^\circ - \sin 0^\circ)/(\cos 90^\circ - \cos 60^\circ)$.

    a. -1/2

    b. 2/3

    c. 0

    d. 1/2

45. Consider 2 triangles, ABC and A'B'C', where:

    BC = B' C'

    AC = A' C'

    RA = RA'

Are these 2 triangles congruent?

    a. Yes

    b. No

    c. Not enough information

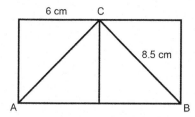

Note: Figure not drawn to scale

46. Assuming the 2 quadrangles are identical rectangles, what is the perimeter of △ABC in the above shape?

 a. 25.5 cm

 b. 27 cm

 c. 30 cm

 d. 29 cm

47. Find the cotangent of a right angle.

 a. -1

 b. 0

 c. 1/2

 d. -1/2

48. If angle α is equal to the expression 3π/2 - π/6 - π - π/3, find sinα.

 a. 0

 b. 1/2

 c. 1

 d. 3/2

49. Find x if $\log_x(9/25) = 2$.

    a. 3/5

    b. 5/3

    c. 6/5

    d. 5/6

50. If $a_0 = 1/2$ and $a_n = 2a_{n-1}^2$, find a_2 of the sequence $\{a_n\}$.

    a. 1/2

    b. 1/4

    c. 1/16

    d. 1/24

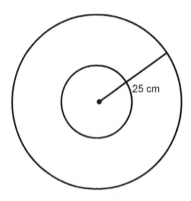

Note: figure not drawn to scale

51. What is the distance travelled by the wheel above, when it makes 175 revolutions?

    a. 87.5 π m

    b. 875 π m

    c. 8.75 π m

    d. 8750 π m

52. If members of the sequence {a_n} are represented by $a_n = (-1)^n a_{n-1}$ and if $a_2 = 2$, find a_0.

    a. 2

    b. 1

    c. 0

    d. -2

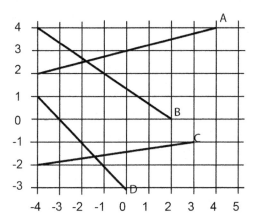

53. Which of the lines above represents the equation $2y - x = 4$?

    a. A

    b. B

    c. C

    d. D

54. For any a, find tga•ctga.

    a. -1

    b. 0

    c. 1/2

    d. 1

Practice the Accuplacer®!

55. If cosα = 3/5 and b = 24, find side c.

  a. 25
  b. 30
  c. 35
  d. 40

56. Find the sides of a right triangle whose sides are consecutive numbers.

  a. 1, 2, 3
  b. 2, 3, 4
  c. 3, 4, 5
  d. 4, 5, 6

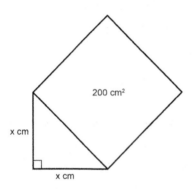

Note: figure not drawn to scale

57. Assuming the quadrangle is square, what is the length of the sides in the triangle above?

  a. 10
  b. 20
  c. 100
  d. 40

58. Calculate (cos(π/2) + ctg(π/2))/sin(π/2).

    a. -2

    b. -1

    c. 0

    d. 1/2

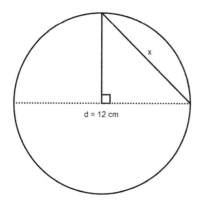

Note: figure not drawn to scale

59. Calculate the length of side x.

    a. 6.46

    b. 8.48

    c. 3.6

    d. 6.4

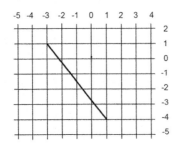

60. What is the slope of the line shown above?

    a. 5/4
    b. -4/5
    c. -5/4
    d. -4/5

Sentence Skills

Directions: Select the best option to replace the under-lined portion of the sentence.

1. If Joe had told me the truth, <u>I wouldn't have been</u> so angry.

    a. No change is necessary

    b. If Joe would have told me the truth, I wouldn't have been so angry.

    c. I wouldn't have been so angry if Joe would have told the truth.

    d. If Joe would have telled me the truth, I wouldn't have been so angry.

2. Although you may <u>not see nobody in the dark, it does</u> <u>not mean that not nobody</u> is there.

    a. Although you may not see nobody in the dark, it does not mean that nobody is there.

    b. Although you may not see anyone in the dark, it does not mean that not nobody is there.

    c. Although you may not see anyone in the dark, it does not mean that anyone is there.

    d. No change is necessary.

3. The Ford Motor Company was named for Henry Ford, <u>whom</u> had founded the company.

    a. The Ford Motor Company was named for Henry Ford, which had founded the company.

    b. The Ford Motor Company was named for Henry Ford, who founded the company.

    c. The Ford Motor Company was named for Henry Ford, whose had founded the company.

    d. No change is necessary.

4. Thomas Edison <u>will had been known</u> as the greatest inventor since he invented the light bulb, television, motion pictures, and phonograph.

    a. Thomas Edison has always been known as the greatest inventor since he invented the light bulb, television, motion pictures, and phonograph.

    b. Thomas Edison was always been known as the greatest inventor since he invented the light bulb, television, motion pictures, and phonograph.

    c. Thomas Edison must have had been always known as the greatest inventor since he invented the light bulb, television, motion pictures, and phonograph.

    d. No change is necessary.

5. The weatherman on Channel 6 said that this has been the hottest summer on record.

    a. The weatherman on Channel 6 said that this has been the most hotter summer on record

    b. The weatherman on Channel 6 said that this has been the most hottest summer on record

    c. The weatherman on Channel 6 said that this has been the hotter summer on record

    d. No change is necessary.

6. Although Joe is tall for his age, his brother Elliot is the tallest of the two.

    a. Although Joe is tall for his age, his brother Elliot is more tallest of the two.

    b. Although Joe is tall for his age, his brother Elliot is the tall the two.

    c. Although Joe is tall for his age, his brother Elliot is the taller of the two.

    d. No change is necessary

7. When KISS came to town, all the tickets was sold out before I could buy one.

    a. When KISS came to town, all the tickets will be sold out before I could buy one.

    b. When KISS came to town, all the tickets had been sold out before I could buy one.

    c. When KISS came to town, all the tickets were being sold out before I could buy one.

    d. No change is necessary.

8. The rules of most sports <u>has been</u> more complicated than we often realize.

a. The rules of most sports are more complicated than we often realize.

b. The rules of most sports is more complicated than we often realize.

c. The rules of most sports was more complicated than we often realize.

d. No change is necessary.

9. Neither of the Wright Brothers <u>had any doubts</u> that they would be successful with their flying machine.

a. Neither of the Wright Brothers have any doubts that they would be successful with their flying machine.

b. Neither of the Wright Brothers has any doubts that they would be successful with their flying machine.

c. Neither of the Wright Brothers had any doubts that they would be successful with their flying machine.

d. No change is necessary.

10. The Titanic <u>has already sunk</u> mere days into its maiden voyage.

a. The Titanic will already sunk mere days into its maiden voyage.

b. The Titanic already sank mere days into its maiden voyage.

c. The Titanic sank mere days into its maiden voyage.

d. No change is necessary.

11. The second act was followed by an intermission.

Rewrite, beginning with

An intermission

The next words will be

      a. came after the second act
      b. was followed by the second act
      c. following the second act
      d. came before the second act

12. As he was boarding the plane, Thomas discovered that he had forgotten his toothbrush.

Rewrite, beginning with

Thomas was boarding the plane

The next words will be

      a. as he was discovering
      b. as he had forgotten
      c. when he forgot
      d. when he discovered

13. Because of the wild coyotes, they built a fence for their puppy.

Rewrite, beginning with

They built a fence

The next words will be

      a. because of the puppy
      b. to protect their puppy from
      c. for their wild coyote
      d. because to protect

14. The more time you invest in learning a second language, the more enjoyable it becomes.

Rewrite, beginning with

Learning a second language becomes more enjoyable

The next words will be

     a. the more investing

     b. as you invest more

     c. and the more you

     d. but you invest more

15. It is annoying, but necessary to own a cell phone.

Rewrite, beginning with

While necessary,

The next words will be

     a. it is annoying to

     b. but owning a cell phone

     c. owning a cell phone

     d. cell phones are

16. The stolen car speeded down the highway without any headlights.

Rewrite, beginning with

Although the stolen car didn't have any headlights,

The next words will be

     a. down the highway it

     b. nonetheless speeding down

     c. and it speeded down

     d. it speeded down

17. Without the right tools, Jess cannot fix her bike.

Rewrite, beginning with

Jess cannot fix her bike

The next words will be

    a. with the right

    b. unless she has the right

    c. if she has the right

    d. having the right

18. Boring through the first three chapters, the book becomes exciting in the fourth.

Rewrite, beginning with

The book becomes exciting

The next words will be

    a. after the first three

    b. until the fourth

    c. after the fourth

    d. before the fourth

19. Simon didn't smell any roses as he walked through the garden.

Rewrite, beginning with

Walking through the garden,

The next words will be

    a. no roses could be smelled

    b. but Simon didn't smell any roses

    c. but smelling no roses

    d. Simon didn't smell any roses.

20. Howard applied sunscreen because he has sensitive skin.

Rewrite, beginning with

Since he has sensitive skin,

The next words will be

   a. sunscreen
   b. Howard applied
   c. applying
   d. because Howard applied

Answer Key

Reading

1. B
The correct answer because that fact is stated directly in the passage. The passage explains that Anne taught Helen to hear by allowing her to feel the vibrations in her throat.

2. A
We can infer that Anne is a patient teacher because she did not leave or lose her temper when Helen bit or hit her; she just kept trying to teach Helen. Choice B is incorrect because Anne taught Helen to read and talk. Choice C is incorrect because Anne could hear. She was partially blind, not deaf. Choice D is incorrect because it does not have to do with patience.

3. B
The passage states that it was hard for anyone but Anne to understand Helen when she spoke. Choice A is incorrect because the passage does not mention Helen spoke a foreign language. Choice C is incorrect because there is no mention of how quiet or loud Helen's voice was. Choice D is incorrect because we know from reading the passage that Helen did learn to speak.

4. D
This question tests the reader's summarization skills. The other choices A, B, and C focus on portions of the second paragraph that are too narrow and do not relate to the specific portion of text in question. The complexity of the sentence may mislead students into selecting one of these answers, but rearranging or restating the sentence will lead the reader to the correct answer. In addition, choice A makes an assumption that may or may not be true about the intentions of the company, choice B focuses on one product rather than the idea of the products, and choice C makes an assumption about women that may or may not be true and is not supported by the text.

5. C
The cumulus stage of a thunderstorm is the beginning of the

thunderstorm.

This is taken directly from the passage, "The first stage of a thunderstorm is the cumulus, or developing stage."

6. D
The passage lists four ways that air is heated. One way is, heat created by water vapor condensing into liquid.

7. A
The sequence of events can be taken from these sentences:

As the moisture carried by the [1] air currents rises, it rapidly cools into liquid drops of water, which appear as cumulus clouds. As the water vapor condenses into liquid, it [2] releases heat, which warms the air. This in turn causes the air to become less dense than the surrounding dry air and [3] rise farther.

8. B
The correct answer can be found in the fourth sentence of the first paragraph.

Option A is incorrect because repenting begins the day AFTER Mardi Gras. Option C is incorrect because you can celebrate Mardi Gras without being a member of a Krewe.

Option D is incorrect because exploration does not play any role in a modern Mardi Gras celebration.

9. A
The second sentence is the last paragraph states that Krewes are led by the Kings and Queens. Therefore, you must have to be part of a Krewe to be its King or its Queen.

Option B is incorrect because it never states in the passage that only people from France can be Kings and Queen of Mardi Gras. Option C is incorrect because the passage says nothing about having to speak French. Option D is incorrect because the passage does state that the Kings and Queens throw doubloons, which is fake money.

10. C

The first sentences of BOTH the 2nd and 3rd paragraphs mention that French explorers started this tradition in New Orleans.

Options A, B and D are incorrect because they are just names of cities or countries listed in the 2nd paragraph.

11. D

Clouds in space are made of different materials attracted by gravity. Clouds on Earth are made of water droplets or ice crystals.

Choice D is the best answer. Notice also that Choice D is the most specific.

12. C

The main idea is the first sentence of the passage; a cloud is a visible mass of droplets or frozen crystals floating in the atmosphere above the surface of the Earth or other planetary body.

The main idea is very often the first sentence of the paragraph.

13. C

This question asks about the process, and gives choices that can be confirmed or eliminated easily.

From the passage, "Dense, deep clouds reflect most light, so they appear white, at least from the top. Cloud droplets scatter light very efficiently, so the farther into a cloud light travels, the weaker it gets. This accounts for the gray or dark appearance at the base of large clouds."

We can eliminate choice A, since water droplets inside the cloud do not reflect light is false.

We can eliminate choice B, since, water droplets outside the cloud reflect light, it appears dark, is false.

Choice C is correct.

14. B
The general tone is informal.

15. B
The statement, " Fewer people have aquariums in their office than at home," cannot be inferred from this article.

16. C
The author does not provide evidence for this statement.

17. B
The following statement is an opinion, " Aquarium gravel improves the aesthetics of the aquarium."

18. D
This question tests the reader's summarization skills. The question is asking very generally about the message of the passage, and the title, "Ways Characters Communicate in Theater," is one indication of that. The other choices A, B, and C are all directly from the text, and therefore readers may be inclined to select one of them, but are too specific to encapsulate the entirety of the passage and its message.

19. B
The paragraph on soliloquies mentions "To be or not to be," and it is from the context of that paragraph that readers may understand that because "To be or not to be" is a soliloquy, Hamlet will be introspective, or thoughtful, while delivering it. It is true that actors deliver soliloquies alone, and may be "solitary" (choice A), but "thoughtful" (choice B) is more true to the overall idea of the paragraph. Readers may choose C because drama and theater can be used interchangeably and the passage mentions that soliloquies are unique to theater (and therefore drama), but this answer is not specific enough to the paragraph in question. Readers may pick up on the theme of life and death and Hamlet's true intentions and select that he is "hopeless" (choice D), but those themes are not discussed either by this paragraph or passage, as a close textual reading and analysis confirms.

20. C
This question tests the reader's grammatical skills. Choice B seems logical, but parenthesis are actually considered to be a stronger break in a sentence than commas are, and along

this line of thinking, actually disrupt the sentence more.

Choices A and D make comparisons between theater and film that are simply not made in the passage, and may or may not be true. This detail does clarify the statement that asides are most unique to theater by adding that it is not completely unique to theater, which may have been why the author didn't chose not to delete it and instead used parentheses to designate the detail's importance (choice C).

21. A
An example of a cold-blooded animal that hibernates underground during the winter is the snake.

Snakes, such as garter snakes and western rattlesnakes, hibernate underground in large groups during the winter.

The second sentence reinforces the first.

The second sentence reinforces the first with supporting details.

22. C
The dog barked and ran.

The dog barked and ran after the postman who was delivering mail.

The second sentence expands on the first.

The second sentence expands on the first sentence because it expresses in greater detail why the dog barked and ran and who it ran after.

24. D
Aphids, pest commonly found on roses, are destroying my rose bushes.

If I spray my rose bushes with insecticidal soap, I will kill the aphids.

The second sentence proposes a solution for the problem mentioned in the first sentence.

25. C

Ms. Apple received and reviewed her students', who all scored on the 99th percentile, standardized test results.

She discovered that most of her students performed at the highest level of achievement; thus, they have mastered the material and skills taught.

The second sentence analyzes a statement made in the first (a part of the first sentence).

26. C

Human activities have contributed to global warming.

Due to global warming, hurricanes, tornadoes and other storms will become stronger and more frequent.

The second sentence states an effect of global warming.

27. D

Jungles and rainforests are both associated with tropical climates.

Vegetation in jungles are tangled and impenetrable (hard to walk through without cutting your way through); however, vegetation in the rainforest is sparse.

The second sentence describes the differences between jungles and rainforests whereas the first compares their similarities.

28. B

Rosaline's friend invited her to the Civil Rights Photography Exhibit at the local museum.

Rosaline did not know as much as she wanted to about the African-American Civil Rights Movement, so she went to the library and checked out books related to the African-American Civil Rights Movement.

The second sentence provides a problem and solution.

29. A
Parrots and macaws are beautiful, colorful birds.

There are over 370 species of parrots, but there are only 18 species of macaws.

The second sentence describes the differences between parrots and macaws whereas the first compares their similarities.

30. B
Paris is often called the "City of Lights."

Paris is called the "City of Lights" because there are over 296 illuminated sites and buildings in Paris, and most importantly, Paris was the birthplace of the Age of Enlightenment.

The second sentence reinforces the first sentences claim with supporting details.

Arithmetic

1. C
If there are 5 friends and each drink costs $1.89, we can round up to $2 per drink and estimate the total cost at, 5 X $2 = $10.
The actual, cost is 5 X $1.89 = $9.45.

2. A
2cnx = 2(4 x 5 x 3) =, 2 x 60/2 x 5 =, 120/10 = 12

3. D
75/1500 = 15/300 = 3/60 = 1/20

4. C
16 X 230 is about 3,100. The actual number is 3680.

5. B

Day	Number of Absent Students	Number of Present Students	% Attendance
Monday	5	40	88.88%
Tuesday	9	36	80.00%
Wednesday	4	41	91.11%
Thursday	10	35	77.77%
Friday	6	39	86.66%

To find the average or mean, sum the series and divide by the number of items.
88.88 + 80.00 + 91.11 + 77.77 + 86.66/5
424.42/5 = 84.88
Round up to 85%.

Percentage attendance will be 85%

6. C
Let the original price be 100x.

At the rate of 7% discount, the discount will be 100x•7/100 = 7x. So, the discounted price will be = 100x - 7x = 93x.

Over this price, at the rate of 2% additional discount, the discount will be 93x•2/100 = 1.86x. So, the additionally discounted price will be = 93x - 1.86x = 91.14x.

This is the amount which John has paid for the jacket:

91.14x = 425

x = 425 / 91.14 = 4.6631

The jacket costs 100x. So, 100x = 100•4.6631 = $466.31.

When rounded to the nearest whole number, this is equal to $466.

7. B
215 X 65 is about 13,500. The exact answer is 13,975.

8. C
$10 \times 2 - (7 + 9) = 4$. This is an order of operations question. Do the brackets first, then multiplication and division, then addition and subtraction.

9. B
$40/100 \, X = 90$
$40X = (90 * 100) = 9000$
$x = 9000/40 = 900/4 = 225$
Half of $225 = 112.5$

10. B
First, see if you can eliminate any options. $1/4 + 1/3$ is going to equal about $1/2$.

Option A, $9/10$ is very close to 1, so it can be eliminated. Options B and C are very close to $1/2$ so they should be considered. Option D is less than half and very close to zero, so it can be eliminated.

Looking at the denominators, option C has denominator of 15, and option B has denominator of 20. Right away, notice that 20 is common multiple of 4 and 10, and 15 is not.

11. C
1 inch on map = 2,000 inches on ground. So, 5.2 inches on map = $5.2 \cdot 2,000 = 10,400$ inches on ground.

12. B
Actual cost = X, therefore, $545 = x + 0.15x$, $545 = 1x + 0.15x$, $545 = 1.15x$, $x = 545/1.15 = 473.9$

13. C
$0.27 + 0.33 = 0.60$ and $0.60 = 60/100 = 3/5$

14. D
First, we need to convert all units to grams. Since 1000 g = 1 kg:

10 kg 550 g = $10 \cdot 1000$ g + 550 g = 10,000 g + 550 g = 10,550 g.

10,550 g is shared between 5 men. So each man will have to carry $10,550/5 = 2,110$ g

2,110 g = 2,000 g + 110 g = 2 kg 110 g

15. D
A common denominator is needed, a number which both 4 and 16 will divide into. So, 4+11/16 = 15/16

16. B
As the lawn is square , the length of one side will be the square root of the area. $\sqrt{62,500}$ = 250 meters. So, the perimeter is found by 4 times the length of the side of the square:

250•4 = 1000 meters.

Since each meter costs $5.5, the total cost of the fence will be 1000•5.5 = $5,500.

17. A
The easiest way to solve age problems is to use a table:

	Mother	Child
Now	7x	x
25 years later	7x + 25	x + 25

Now, mother is 7 times older than her child. So, if we say that the child is x years old, mother is 7x years old. In 25 years, 25 will be added to their ages. We are told that in 25 years, mother's age will double her child's age. So,

7x + 25 = 2(x + 25) ... by solving this equation, we reach x that is the child's age:

7x + 25 = 2x + 50

7x - 2x = 50 - 25

5x = 25

x = 5

Mother is 7x years old: 7x = 7•5 = 35

18. A
0.28 = 28/100 = 7/25

19. C

By the given information in the question, we understand that the discounted part is the saved amount. If we say that the original price of the desk is 100x; by 20% discount rate, 20x will be the discounted part:

20x = 45

We know that Mark paid 20% less than the original price. So, he paid 100x - 20x = 80x. We are asked to find 80x. With a simple direct proportion, we can find the result:

20x = 45

<u>80x = ?</u>

By cross multiplication, we find the result:

? = 80x•45 / 20x = 4•45 = $180

20. C

Let the number be x.

x/(3/2) is the required result.

x•(3/2) is the operation the student does mistakenly. We are told that the multiplication result is 5 more than the division result that is the required one:

x•(3/2) = x/(3/2) + 5 ... by solving this equation, we find x.

3x/2 = 2x/3 + 5

3x/2 - 2x/3 = 5 ... by equating the denominators to 6:

9x/6 - 4x/6 = 5

(9x - 4x)/6 = 5

5x/6 = 5

5x = 30

x = 6

Algebra

21. C
243/(3 x 3 x 3) = 243/27 = 9

22. B
4y + 24 = 3y + 30, = 4y – 3y + 24 = 30, = y + 24 = 30, = y = 30 – 24, = y = 6

23. B
$(x^2 - y^2) / (x - y) = x + y$

$$\frac{-(x^2 - xy)}{xy - y^2}$$

$$\frac{-(xy - y^2)}{0}$$

24. A
10 x 10 x 100 x 100 = 1000^x, =100 x 10,000 = 1000^x, = 1,000,000 = 1000^x = x = 2

25. C
We are asked to find A + B - C. By paying attention to the sign distribution; we write the polynomials and operate:

A + B - C = $(-2x^4 + x^2 - 3x) + (x^4 - x^3 + 5) - (x^4 + 2x^3 + 4x + 5)$

= $-2x^4 + x^2 - 3x + x^4 - x^3 + 5 - x^4 - 2x^3 - 4x - 5$

= $-2x^4 + x^4 - x^4 - x^3 - 2x^3 + x^2 - 3x - 4x + 5 - 5$ ... similar terms written together to ease summing/substituting.

= $-2x^4 - 3x^3 + x^2 - 7x$

26. C
To find the solution for the inequality, we need to simplify it first:

$(x - 6)^2 \geq x^2 + 12$ ... we can write the open form of the left side:

$x^2 - 12x + 36 \geq x^2 + 12$ ... x^2 terms on both sides cancel each other:

-12x + 36 ≥ 12 ... Now, we aim to have x alone on one side. So, we subtract 36 from both sides:

-12x + 36 - 36 ≥ 12 - 36

-12x ≥ -24 ... We divide both sides by -12. This means that the inequality will change its direction:

$x \leq 2$ ... x can be 2 or a smaller value.

This result is shown by (-∞, 2].

27. B
(7 x 7 x 7 x 7 x 7) - (3 x 3 x 3 x 3 x 3) = 16,807 – 243 = 16,564.

28. C
$(x^3 - 3x^2 + 3x - 1) / (x - 1) = x^2 - 2x + 1$
$\underline{-(x^3 - x^2)}$
$\quad\ -2x^2 + 3x - 1$
$\underline{\ -(-2x^2 + 2x)}$
$\qquad\qquad x - 1$

$\underline{-(x - 1)}$
0

29. C
Exponential form is 9^3 and standard from is 729

30. B
$x^2 - 5x - 6 = 0$

We try to separate the middle term -5x to find common factors with x^2 and -6 separately:

$x^2 - 6x + x - 6 = 0$ ... Here, we see that x is a common factor for x^2 and -6x:

x(x - 6) + x - 6 = 0 ... Here, we have x times x - 6 and 1 time x - 6 summed up. This means that we have x + 1 times x - 6:

(x + 1)(x - 6) = 0 ... This is true when either or both of the expressions in the parenthesis are equal to zero:

x + 1 = 0 ... x = -1

x - 6 = 0 ... x = 6

-1 and 6 are the solutions for this quadratic equation.

31. B

0.524/ (10•10•10) = 0.524/1000 ... This means that we need to carry the decimal point 3 decimals left from the point it is now:

= 0.0.0.0.524 = 0.000524

The correct answer is (b).

32. A

We need to find the greatest common divisor of the two terms in order to factor the expression. We should remember that if the bases of exponent numbers are the same, the multiplication of two terms is found by summing the powers and writing on the same base. Similarly; when dividing, the power of the divisor is subtracted from the power of the divided.

Both x^3y^3 and x^2y^8 contain x^2 and y^3. So;

$x^3y^3 - x^2y^8 = x•x^2y^3 - y^5•x^2y^3$ ... We can carry x^2y^3 out as the factor:

$= x^2y^3(x - y^5)$

33. D

Our aim to collect the knowns on one side and the unknowns (x terms) on the other side:

$5x/2 = (3x + 24)/6$ ... First, we can simplify the denominators of both sides by 2:

$5x = (3x + 24)/3$ ... Now, we can do cross multiplication:

$15x = 3x + 24$

$15x - 3x = 24$

$12x = 24$

$x = 24/12 = 2$

34. D
When multiplying exponents with the same base, add the
exponents. $3^2 \times 3^5 = 3^{2+5} = 3^7$

35. C
Solving the system means finding x and y. Since we also
have a in the system, we will find x and y depending on a.

We can obtain y by using the equation $ax + y = 1$:

$y = 1 - ax$ ... Then, we can insert this value into the second
equation:

$x + a(1 - ax) = 1$

$x + a - a^2x = 1$

$x - a^2x = 1 - a$

$x(1 - a^2) = 1 - a$ ... We need to obtain x alone:

$x = (1 - a)/(1 - a^2)$ ... Here, $1 - a^2 = (1 - a)(1 + a)$ is used:

$x = (1 - a)/((1 - a)(1 + a))$ ... Simplifying by $(1 - a)$:

$x = 1/(a + 1)$ ... Now we know the value of x. By using either
of the equations, we can find the value of y. Let us use $y =
1 - ax$:

$y = 1 - a \bullet 1/(a + 1)$

$y = 1 - a/(a + 1)$ ... By writing on the same denominator:

$y = ((a + 1) - a)/(a + 1)$

$y = (a + 1 - a)/(a + 1)$ ... a and -a cancel each other:

$y = 1/(a + 1)$ ... x and y are found to be equal.

The solution of the system is $(1/(a + 1), 1/(a + 1))$

36. A
To divide exponents with the same base, subtract the exponents. $3^{8-5} = 3^3$

37. C
To solve the linear equation, we operate the knowns and
unknowns within each other and try to obtain x term (which

is the unknown) alone on one side of the equation:

$3(x + 2) - 2(1 - x) = 4x + 5$ ... We remove the parenthesis by distributing the factors:

$3x + 6 - 2 + 2x = 4x + 5$

$5x + 4 = 4x + 5$

$5x - 4x = 5 - 4$

$x = 1$

38. C
$3x^a + 6a^x - x^a + (-5a^x) - 2x^a = 3x^a + 6a^x - x^a - 5a^x - 2x^a = a^x$

39. B
By paying attention to the sign distribution; we write the polynomials and operate:
$(-3x^2 + 2x + 6) + (-x^2 - x - 1)$

$= -3x^2 + 2x + 6 - x^2 - x - 1$

$= -3x^2 - x^2 + 2x - x + 6 - 1$ ... similar terms written together to ease summing/substituting.

$= -4x^2 + x + 5$

40. A
10^4 is not equal to $100,000$
$10^4 = 10 \times 10 \times 10 \times 10 = 10^2 \times 10^2 = 10,000$

College Level

41. D
Comparing angles on similar triangles, a, b and c will be $70°$, $35°$, $35°$

42. D
$\log_x 125 = 3$ ... we use the property that $\log_a a^b = b \cdot \log_a a = b$

$\log_x 125 = 3 \cdot \log_x x$

$\log_x 125 = \log_x x^3$ ... We can cancel the $\log_x$ function on both sides:

$125 = x^3$

$5^3 = x^3$

$5 = x$

So; x = 5

43. C
$(1 - 4\sin^2(\pi/6))/(1+4\cos^2(\pi/3)) = (1 - 4\sin^2(30°))/(1 + 4\cos^2(60°))$

We know that sin30° = cos60° = 1/2

$(1 - 4\sin^2(30°))/(1 + 4\cos^2(60°)) = (1 - 4•(1/2)^2)/(1 + 4•(1/2)^2)$

$= (1 - 4•(1/4))/(1 + 4•(1/4))$

$= (1 - 1)/(1 + 1) = 0/2 = 0$

44. A
We know that sin30° = cos60° = 1/2, sin0° = cos90° = 0
$(\sin^2 30° - \sin 0°)/(\cos 90° - \cos 60°) = ((1/2)^2 - 0)/(0 - (1/2))$

$= (1/4)/(-1/2) = -1/2$

45. A
Yes the triangles are congruent.

46. D
Perimeter of triangle ABC is asked.
Perimeter of a triangle = sum of all three sides.

Here, Perimeter of ΔABC = |AC| + |CB| + |AB|.

Since the triangle is located in the middle of two adjacent and identical rectangles, we find the side lengths using these rectangles:

|AB| = 6 + 6 = 12 cm

|CB| = 8.5 cm

|AC| = |CB| = 8.5 cm

Perimeter = $|AC| + |CB| + |AB| = 8.5 + 8.5 + 12 = 29$ cm

47. B

$a = 90°$

$\cot 90° = \cos 90° / \sin 90° = 0/1 = 0$

48. A

First, we need to simplify the value of angle a:

$a = 3\pi/2 - \pi/6 - \pi - \pi/3$ ... by equating the denominators at 6:

$a = 9\pi/6 - \pi/6 - 6\pi/6 - 2\pi/6$

$a = (9 - 1 - 6 - 2)\pi/6$

$a = 0 \cdot \pi/6$

$a = 0$

$\sin a = \sin 0° = 0$

49. A

$\log_x(9/25) = 2$ ... we use the property that $\log_a a^b = b \cdot \log_a a = b$

$\log_x(9/25) = 2 \cdot \log_x x$

$\log_x(9/25) = \log_x x^2$ ... We can cancel the $\log_x$ function on both sides:

$9/25 = x^2$

$(3/5)^2 = x^2$ ... We can remove the power 2 in both sides:

$3/5 = x$

So; $x = 3/5$

50. A

We are given that,

$a_0 = 1/2$

$a_n = 2a_{n-1}^2$

Starting from the zeroth term, we can reach the second term:

$n = 1$ ... $a_1 = 2a_0^2 = 2(1/2)^2 = 2(1/4) = 1/2$

$n = 2 \ldots a_2 = 2a_1^2 = 2(1/2)^2 = 2(1/4) = 1/2$

51. A

The wheel travels $2\pi r$ distance when it makes one revolution. Here, r stands for the radius. The radius is given as 25 cm in the figure. So,
$2\pi r = 2\pi \cdot 25 = 50\pi$ cm is the distance travelled in one revolution.

In 175 revolutions: $175 \cdot 50\pi = 8750\pi$ cm is travelled.

We are asked to find the distance in meter.

1 m = 100 cm So;

8750π cm = 8750π / 100 = 87.5π m

52. D

We are given that,

$a_n = (-1)^n a_{n-1}$

$a_2 = 2$

Starting from the second term, we can reach the zeroth term in the reverse direction:

$n = 2 \ldots a_2 = (-1)^2 a_1 \ldots 2 = a_1$

$n = 1 \ldots a_1 = (-1)^1 a_0 \ldots 2 = -a_0 \ldots a_0 = -2$

53. A

If a line represents an equation, all points on that line should satisfy the equation. Meaning that all (x, y) pairs present on the line should be able to verify that 2y - x is equal to 4. We can find out the correct line by trying a (x, y) point existing on each line. It is easier to choose points on the intersection of the gridlines:

Let us try the point (4, 4) on line A:

$2 \cdot 4 - 4 = 4$

$8 - 4 = 4$

$4 = 4$ ... this is a correct result, so the equation for line A is

2y - x = 4.

Let us try other points to check the other lines:

Point (-1, 2) on line B:

2•2 - (-1) = 4

4 + 1 = 4

5 = 4 ... this is a wrong result, so the equation for line B is not 2y - x = 4.

Point (3, -1) on line C:

2•(-1) - 3 = 4

-2 - 3 = 4

-5 = 4 ... this is a wrong result, so the equation for line C is not 2y - x = 4.

Point (-2, -1) on line D:

2•(-1) - (-2) = 4

-2 + 2 = 4

0 = 4 ... this is a wrong result, so the equation for line D is not 2y - x = 4.

54. D
We know that;

tga = sina/cosa

ctga = cosa/sina

So;

tga/ctga = (sina/cosa)•(cosa/sina) = (sina • cosa)/(sina • cosa)

sina terms and cosa terms cancel each other in the nominator and the denominator:

tga/ctga = 1

55. D

To understand this question better, let us draw a right triangle by writing the given data on it:

The side opposite to angle α is named by a.

cos α = length of the adjacent side / length of the hypotenuse = b/c

cos α = 3/5 is given. This means that b/c = 3/5

b = 24 is also given:

24/c = 3/5 ... By cross multiplication:

24•5 = 3c ... Simplifying both sides by 3:

8•5 = c

c = 40

56. C

In a right angle, Pythagorean Theorem is applicable:
$a^2 + b^2 = c^2$ ... Here, a and b represent the adjacent and opposite sides, c represents the hypotenuse. Hypotenuse is larger than the other two sides.

In this question, we need to try each answer choice by applying $a^2 + b^2 = c^2$ to see if it is satisfied; by inserting the largest number into c:

a. 1, 2, 3:

$1^2 + 2^2 = 3^2$

1 + 4 = 9

5 = 9 ... This is not correct, so answer choice does not represent a right angle whose sides are consecutive numbers.

b. 2, 3, 4:

$2^2 + 3^2 = 4^2$

$4 + 9 = 16$

$13 = 16$ ... This is not correct, so this answer choice does not represent a right angle whose sides are consecutive numbers.

c. 3, 4, 5:

$3^2 + 4^2 = 5^2$

$9 + 16 = 25$

$25 = 25$ ... This is correct, 3, 4, 5 are also consecutive numbers; so this answer choice represents a right angle whose sides are consecutive numbers.

d. 4, 5, 6:

$4^2 + 5^2 = 6^2$

$16 + 25 = 36$

$41 = 36$ ... This is not correct, so this answer choice does not represent a right angle whose sides are consecutive numbers.

57. A
If we call one side of the square "a," the area of the square will be a^2.

We know that $a^2 = 200$ cm^2.

On the other hand; there is an isosceles right triangle. Using the Pythagorean Theorem:

(Hypotenuse)^2 = (Perpendicular)^2 + (Base)^2
$h^2 = a^2 + b^2$

Given: $h^2 = 200$, $a = b = x$
Then, $x^2 + x^2 = 200$, $2x^2 = 200$, $x^2 = 100$
$x = 10$

58. C
We know that $\pi/2 = 90°$

$\cos 90° = 0$, $\sin 90° = 1$

$\operatorname{ctg} 90° = \cos 90° / \sin 90° = 0/1 = 0$ So;

$(\cos(\pi/2) + \operatorname{ctg}(\pi/2))/\sin(\pi/2) = (\cos 90° + \operatorname{ctg} 90°)/\sin 90° = (0 + 0)/1 = 0$

59. B

In the question, we have a right triangle formed inside the circle. We are asked to find the length of the hypotenuse of this triangle. We can find the other two sides of the triangle by using circle properties:

The diameter of the circle is equal to 12 cm. The legs of the right triangle are the radii of the circle; so they are 6 cm long.

Using the Pythagorean Theorem:

$(\text{Hypotenuse})^2 = (\text{Perpendicular})^2 + (\text{Base})^2$
$h^2 = a^2 + b^2$

Given: d (diameter)= 12 & r (radius) = a = b = 6
$h^2 = a^2 + b^2$
$h^2 = 6^2 + 6^2$, $h^2 = 36 + 36$
$h^2 = 72$
$h = \sqrt{72}$
$h = 8.48$

60. C

Slope (m) = $\dfrac{\text{change in y}}{\text{change in x}}$

$(x_1, y_1)=(-3,1)$ & $(x_2, y_2)= (1,-4)$
Slope $= [-4 - 1]/[1-(-3)]= -5/4$

Sentence Skills

1. A

The third conditional is used for talking about an unreal situation (that did not happen) in the past. For example,

"If I had studied harder, [if clause] I would have passed the exam [main clause]. Which is the same as, "I failed the exam, because I didn't study hard enough."

2. C
Double negative sentence. In double negative sentences, one of the negatives is replaced with "any."

3. B
The sentence refers to a person, so "who" is the only correct option.

4. A
The sentence requires the past perfect "has always been known." Furthermore, this is the only grammatically correct choice.

5. B
The superlative, "hottest," is used when expressing a temperature greater than that of anything to which it is being compared.

6. C
When comparing two items, use "the taller." When comparing more than two items, use "the tallest."

7. B
The past perfect form is used to describe an event that occurred in the past and prior to another event.

8. A
The subject is "rules" so the present tense plural form, "are," is used to agree with "realize."

9. C
The simple past tense, "had," is correct because it refers to completed action in the past.

10. C
The simple past tense, "sank," is correct because it refers to completed action in the past.

11. A
The order must be: second act, and then intermission.

"Came after" is the only synonym of "followed."

12. D
Thomas discovered not gradually, but suddenly: hence "when" instead of "as."

13. B
"To protect their puppy from wild coyotes" combines "because of the wild coyotes" and "for their puppy" while preserving the original meaning.

14. B
"As you invest more" retains the parallel structure grammatically.

15. C
"Necessary" must modify "owning"; "while" already replaces "but."

16. D
The main clause must start with the main subject, "it." No conjunction is needed in addition to "although."

17. B
The only phrase that preserves the use of "without" is "unless."

18. A
The correct sequence is, boring for the first three chapters, then exciting. So, the book is not exciting until after the first three chapters.

19. D
The main clause must begin with "Simon," the main subject, which is modified by "walking."

20. B
"Since" replaces "because" as the subordinating conjunction. The main clause must begin with "Howard."

Practice Test Questions Set 2

The questions below are not the same as you will find on the Accuplacer® - that would be too easy! And nobody knows what the questions will be and they change all the time. Below are general questions that cover the same subject areas as the Accuplacer®. So, while the format and exact wording of the questions may differ slightly, and change from year to year, if you can answer the questions below, you will have no problem with the Accuplacer®.

For the best results, take these Practice Test Questions as if it were the real exam. Set aside time when you will not be disturbed, and a location that is quiet and free of distractions. Read the instructions carefully, read each question carefully, and answer to the best of your ability.
Use the bubble answer sheets provided. When you have completed the Practice Questions, check your answer against the Answer Key and read the explanation provided.

Do not attempt more than one set of practice test questions in one day. After completing the first practice test, wait two or three days before attempting the second set of questions.

Practice the Accuplacer®!

Reading Answer Sheet

1. (A) (B) (C) (D)   11. (A) (B) (C) (D)   21. (A) (B) (C) (D)

2. (A) (B) (C) (D)   12. (A) (B) (C) (D)   22. (A) (B) (C) (D)

3. (A) (B) (C) (D)   13. (A) (B) (C) (D)   23. (A) (B) (C) (D)

4. (A) (B) (C) (D)   14. (A) (B) (C) (D)   24. (A) (B) (C) (D)

5. (A) (B) (C) (D)   15. (A) (B) (C) (D)   25. (A) (B) (C) (D)

6. (A) (B) (C) (D)   16. (A) (B) (C) (D)   26. (A) (B) (C) (D)

7. (A) (B) (C) (D)   17. (A) (B) (C) (D)   27. (A) (B) (C) (D)

8. (A) (B) (C) (D)   18. (A) (B) (C) (D)   28. (A) (B) (C) (D)

9. (A) (B) (C) (D)   19. (A) (B) (C) (D)   29. (A) (B) (C) (D)

10. (A) (B) (C) (D)   20. (A) (B) (C) (D)   30. (A) (B) (C) (D)

Mathematics Answer Sheet
(Arithmetic, Algebra and College Level Math)

1. Ⓐ Ⓑ Ⓒ Ⓓ 21. Ⓐ Ⓑ Ⓒ Ⓓ 41. Ⓐ Ⓑ Ⓒ Ⓓ

2. Ⓐ Ⓑ Ⓒ Ⓓ 22. Ⓐ Ⓑ Ⓒ Ⓓ 42. Ⓐ Ⓑ Ⓒ Ⓓ

3. Ⓐ Ⓑ Ⓒ Ⓓ 23. Ⓐ Ⓑ Ⓒ Ⓓ 43. Ⓐ Ⓑ Ⓒ Ⓓ

4. Ⓐ Ⓑ Ⓒ Ⓓ 24. Ⓐ Ⓑ Ⓒ Ⓓ 44. Ⓐ Ⓑ Ⓒ Ⓓ

5. Ⓐ Ⓑ Ⓒ Ⓓ 25. Ⓐ Ⓑ Ⓒ Ⓓ 45. Ⓐ Ⓑ Ⓒ Ⓓ

6. Ⓐ Ⓑ Ⓒ Ⓓ 26. Ⓐ Ⓑ Ⓒ Ⓓ 46. Ⓐ Ⓑ Ⓒ Ⓓ

7. Ⓐ Ⓑ Ⓒ Ⓓ 27. Ⓐ Ⓑ Ⓒ Ⓓ 47. Ⓐ Ⓑ Ⓒ Ⓓ

8. Ⓐ Ⓑ Ⓒ Ⓓ 28. Ⓐ Ⓑ Ⓒ Ⓓ 48. Ⓐ Ⓑ Ⓒ Ⓓ

9. Ⓐ Ⓑ Ⓒ Ⓓ 29. Ⓐ Ⓑ Ⓒ Ⓓ 49. Ⓐ Ⓑ Ⓒ Ⓓ

10. Ⓐ Ⓑ Ⓒ Ⓓ 30. Ⓐ Ⓑ Ⓒ Ⓓ 50. Ⓐ Ⓑ Ⓒ Ⓓ

11. Ⓐ Ⓑ Ⓒ Ⓓ 31. Ⓐ Ⓑ Ⓒ Ⓓ 51. Ⓐ Ⓑ Ⓒ Ⓓ

12. Ⓐ Ⓑ Ⓒ Ⓓ 32. Ⓐ Ⓑ Ⓒ Ⓓ 52. Ⓐ Ⓑ Ⓒ Ⓓ

13. Ⓐ Ⓑ Ⓒ Ⓓ 33. Ⓐ Ⓑ Ⓒ Ⓓ 53. Ⓐ Ⓑ Ⓒ Ⓓ

14. Ⓐ Ⓑ Ⓒ Ⓓ 34. Ⓐ Ⓑ Ⓒ Ⓓ 54. Ⓐ Ⓑ Ⓒ Ⓓ

15. Ⓐ Ⓑ Ⓒ Ⓓ 35. Ⓐ Ⓑ Ⓒ Ⓓ 55. Ⓐ Ⓑ Ⓒ Ⓓ

16. Ⓐ Ⓑ Ⓒ Ⓓ 36. Ⓐ Ⓑ Ⓒ Ⓓ 56. Ⓐ Ⓑ Ⓒ Ⓓ

17. Ⓐ Ⓑ Ⓒ Ⓓ 37. Ⓐ Ⓑ Ⓒ Ⓓ 57. Ⓐ Ⓑ Ⓒ Ⓓ

18. Ⓐ Ⓑ Ⓒ Ⓓ 38. Ⓐ Ⓑ Ⓒ Ⓓ 58. Ⓐ Ⓑ Ⓒ Ⓓ

19. Ⓐ Ⓑ Ⓒ Ⓓ 39. Ⓐ Ⓑ Ⓒ Ⓓ 59. Ⓐ Ⓑ Ⓒ Ⓓ

20. Ⓐ Ⓑ Ⓒ Ⓓ 40. Ⓐ Ⓑ Ⓒ Ⓓ 60. Ⓐ Ⓑ Ⓒ Ⓓ

Sentence Skills Answer Sheet

1. Ⓐ Ⓑ Ⓒ Ⓓ   11. Ⓐ Ⓑ Ⓒ Ⓓ

2. Ⓐ Ⓑ Ⓒ Ⓓ   12. Ⓐ Ⓑ Ⓒ Ⓓ

3. Ⓐ Ⓑ Ⓒ Ⓓ   13. Ⓐ Ⓑ Ⓒ Ⓓ

4. Ⓐ Ⓑ Ⓒ Ⓓ   14. Ⓐ Ⓑ Ⓒ Ⓓ

5. Ⓐ Ⓑ Ⓒ Ⓓ   15. Ⓐ Ⓑ Ⓒ Ⓓ

6. Ⓐ Ⓑ Ⓒ Ⓓ   16. Ⓐ Ⓑ Ⓒ Ⓓ

7. Ⓐ Ⓑ Ⓒ Ⓓ   17. Ⓐ Ⓑ Ⓒ Ⓓ

8. Ⓐ Ⓑ Ⓒ Ⓓ   18. Ⓐ Ⓑ Ⓒ Ⓓ

9. Ⓐ Ⓑ Ⓒ Ⓓ   19. Ⓐ Ⓑ Ⓒ Ⓓ

10. Ⓐ Ⓑ Ⓒ Ⓓ   20. Ⓐ Ⓑ Ⓒ Ⓓ

Part 1 – Reading and Language Arts

Questions 1 - 4 refer to the following passage.

The Civil War

The Civil War began on April 12, 1861. The first shots of the Civil War were fired in Fort Sumter, South Carolina. Note that even though more American lives were lost in the Civil War than in any other war, not one person died on that first day. The war began because eleven Southern states seceded from the Union and tried to start their own government, The Confederate States of America.

Why did the states secede? The issue of slavery was a primary cause of the Civil War. The eleven southern states relied heavily on their slaves to foster their farming and plantation lifestyles. The northern states, many of whom had already abolished slavery, did not think that the southern states should have slaves. The north wanted to free all the slaves and President Lincoln's goal was to both end slavery and preserve the Union. He had Congress declare war on the Confederacy on April 14, 1862. For four long, blood soaked years, the North and South fought.

From 1861 to mid 1863, it seemed as if the South would win this war. However, on July 1, 1863, an epic three day battle was waged on a field in Gettysburg, Pennsylvania. Gettysburg is remembered for being one of the bloodiest battles in American history. At the end of the three days, the North turned the tide of the war in their favor. The North then went onto dominate the South for the remainder of the war. Most well remembered might be General Sherman's "March to The Sea," where he famously led the Union Army through Georgia and the Carolinas, burning and destroying everything in their path.

In 1865, the Union army invaded and captured the Confederate capital of Richmond Virginia. Robert E. Lee, leader of the Confederacy surrendered to General Ulysses S. Grant, leader of the Union forces, on April 9, 1865. The Civil War was over and the Union was preserved.

1. What does secede mean?

    a. To break away from

    b. To accomplish

    c. To join

    d. To lose

2. Which of the following statements summarizes a FACT from the passage?

    a. Congress declared war and then the Battle of Fort Sumter began.

    b. Congress declared war after shots were fired at Fort Sumter.

    c. President Lincoln was pro slavery

    d. President Lincoln was at Fort Sumter with Congress

3. Which event finally led the Confederacy to surrender?

    a. The battle of Gettysburg

    b. The battle of Bull Run

    c. The invasion of the confederate capital of Richmond

    d. Sherman's March to the Sea

4. The word abolish as used in this passage most nearly means?

    a. To ban

    b. To polish

    c. To support

    d. To destroy

Questions 5 - 8 refer to the following passage.

Lightning

Lightning is an electrical discharge that occurs in a thunderstorm. Often you'll see it as a bright "bolt" (or streak) coming from the sky. Lightning occurs when static electricity inside clouds builds up and causes an electrical charge. What causes the static electricity? Water! Specifically, water droplets collide with ice crystals after the temperature in the cloud falls below freezing. Sometimes these collisions are small, but other times they're quite large. Large collisions cause large electrical charges, and when they're large enough, look out! The hyper-charged cloud will emit a burst of lightning. This lightning looks quite impressive. For a good reason, too: A lightning bolt's temperature gets so hot that it's sometimes five times hotter than the sun's surface. Although the lightning bolt is hot, it's also short-lived. Because of that, when a person is unfortunate enough to be struck by lightning, their odds of surviving are pretty good. Statistics show that 90% of victims survive a lightning blast. Oh, and that old saying, "Lightning never strikes twice in the same spot?" It's a myth! Many people report surviving lightning blasts three or more times. What's more, lightning strikes some skyscrapers multiple times. The other prominent feature of lightning storms is the thunder. This is caused by the super-heated air around a lightning bolt expands at the speed of sound. We hear thunder after seeing the lightning bolt because sound travels slower than the speed of light. In reality, though, both occur at the same moment. [3]

5. What can we infer from this passage?

a. An electrical discharge in the clouds causes lightning.

b. Lightning is not as hot as the temperature of the sun's surface.

c. The sound that lightning makes occurs when electricity strikes an object.

d. We hear lightning before we see it.

6. Being struck by lightning means:

a. Instant death.

b. Less than a fifty percent chance of survival.

c. A ninety percent chance of surviving the strike.

d. An eighty percent chance of survival.

7. Lightning is caused by the following:

a. Water droplets colliding with ice crystals creating static electricity.

b. Friction from the clouds rubbing together.

c. Water droplets colliding.

d. Warm and cold air mixing together.

Questions 9 - 12 refer to the following passage.

Low Blood Sugar

As the name suggest, low blood sugar is low sugar levels in the bloodstream. This can occur when you have not eaten properly and undertake strenuous activity, or, when you are very hungry. When Low blood sugar occurs regularly and is ongoing, it is a medical condition called hypoglycemia. This condition can occur in diabetics and in healthy adults.

Causes of low blood sugar can include excessive alcohol consumption, metabolic problems, stomach surgery, pancreas, liver or kidneys problems, as well as a side-effect of some medications.

Symptoms

There are different symptoms depending on the severity of the case.

Mild hypoglycemia can lead to feelings of nausea and hunger. The patient may also feel nervous, jittery and have fast heart beats. Sweaty skin, clammy and cold skin are likely symptoms.

Moderate hypoglycemia can result in a short temper, confusion, nervousness, fear and blurring of vision. The patient may feel weak and unsteady.

Severe cases of hypoglycemia can lead to seizures, coma, fainting spells, nightmares, headaches, excessive sweats and severe tiredness.

Diagnosis of low blood sugar

A doctor can diagnosis this medical condition by asking the patient questions and testing blood and urine samples. Home testing kits are available for patients to monitor blood sugar levels. It is important to see a qualified doctor though. The doctor can administer tests to ensure that will safely rule out other medical conditions that could affect blood sugar levels.

Treatment

Quick treatments include drinking or eating foods and drinks with high sugar contents. Good examples include soda, fruit juice, hard candy and raisins. Glucose energy tablets can also help. Doctors may also recommend medications and well as changes in diet and exercise routine to treat chronic low blood sugar.

9. Based on the article, which of the following is true?

a. Low blood sugar can happen to anyone.

b. Low blood sugar only happens to diabetics.

c. Low blood sugar can occur even.

d. None of the statements are true.

10. Which of the following are the author's opinion?

a. Quick treatments include drinking or eating foods and drinks with high sugar contents.

b. None of the statements are opinions.

c. This condition can occur in diabetics and also in healthy adults.

d. There are different symptoms depending on the severity of the case

11. What is the author's purpose?

a. To inform

b. To persuade

c. To entertain

d. To analyze

12. Which of the following is not a detail?

a. A doctor can diagnosis this medical condition by asking the patient questions and testing.

b. A doctor will test blood and urine samples.

c. Glucose energy tablets can also help.

d. Home test kits monitor blood sugar levels.

Questions 13 - 16 refer to the following passage.

Myths, Legend and Folklore

Cultural historians draw a distinction between myth, legend and folktale simply as a way to group traditional stories. However, in many cultures, drawing a sharp line between myths and legends is not that simple. Instead of dividing their traditional stories into myths, legends, and folktales, some cultures divide them into two categories. The first category roughly corresponds to folktales, and the second is one that combines myths and legends. Similarly, we can not always separate myths from folktales. One society might consider a story true, making it a myth. Another society may believe the story is fiction, which makes it a folktale. In fact, when a myth loses its status as part of a religious system, it often takes on traits more typical of folktales, with its formerly divine characters now appearing as human heroes, giants, or fairies. Myth, legend, and folktale are only a few of the categories of traditional stories. Other categories include anecdotes and some kinds of jokes. Traditional stories, in turn, are only one category within the larger category of folklore, which also includes items such as gestures, costumes, and music. [4]

13. The main idea of this passage is

a. Myths, fables, and folktales are not the same thing, and each describes a specific type of story

b. Traditional stories can be categorized in different ways by different people

c. Cultures use myths for religious purposes, and when this is no longer true, the people forget and discard these myths

d. Myths can never become folk tales, because one is true, and the other is false

14. The terms myth and legend are

a. Categories that are synonymous with true and false

b. Categories that group traditional stories according to certain characteristics

c. Interchangeable, because both terms mean a story that is passed down from generation to generation

d. Meant to distinguish between a story that involves a hero and a cultural message and a story meant only to entertain

15. Traditional story categories not only include myths and legends, but

    a. Can also include gestures, since some cultures passed these down before the written and spoken word

    b. In addition, folklore refers to stories involving fables and fairy tales

    c. These story categories can also include folk music and traditional dress

    d. Traditional stories themselves are a part of the larger category of folklore, which may also include costumes, gestures, and music

16. This passage shows that

    a. There is a distinct difference between a myth and a legend, although both are folktales

    b. Myths are folktales, but folktales are not myths

    c. Myths, legends, and folktales play an important part in tradition and the past, and are a rich and colorful part of history

    d. Most cultures consider myths to be true

Questions 17 - 19 refer to the following passage.

How To Get A Good Nights Sleep

Sleep is just as essential for healthy living as water, air and food. Sleep allows the body to rest and replenish depleted energy levels. Sometimes we may for various reasons experience difficulty sleeping which has a serious effect on our health. Those who have prolonged sleeping problems are facing a serious medical condition and should see a qualified doctor when possible for help. Here is simple guide that can help you sleep better at night.

Try to create a natural pattern of waking up and sleeping around the same time everyday. This means avoiding going to bed too early and oversleeping past your usual wake up time. Going to bed and getting up at radically different times everyday confuses your body clock. Try to establish a natural rhythm as much as you can.

Exercises and a bit of physical activity can help you sleep better at night. If you are having problem sleeping, try to be as active as you can during the day. If you are tired from physical activity, falling asleep is a natural and easy process for your body. If you remain inactive during the day, you will find it harder to sleep properly at night. Try walking, jogging, swimming or simple stretches as you get close to your bed time.

Afternoon naps are great to refresh you during the day, but they may also keep you awake at night. If you feel sleepy during the day, get up, take a walk and get busy to keep from sleeping. Stretching is a good way to increase blood flow to the brain and keep you alert so that you don't sleep during the day. This will help you sleep better night.

> A warm bath or a glass of milk in the evening can help your body relax and prepare for sleep. A cold bath will wake you up and keep you up for several hours. Also avoid eating too late before bed.

17. How would you describe this sentence?

   a. A recommendation

   b. An opinion

   c. A fact

   d. A diagnosis

18. Which of the following is an alternative title for this article?

   a. Exercise and a good night's sleep

   b. Benefits of a good night's sleep

   c. Tips for a good night's sleep

   d. Lack of sleep is a serious medical condition

19. Which of the following cannot be inferred from this article?

a. Biking is helpful for getting a good night's sleep

b. Mental activity is helpful for getting a good night's sleep

c. Eating bedtime snacks is not recommended

d. Getting up at the same time is helpful for a good night's sleep

Directions: For questions 20 to 30 you are given 2 sentences. Select the best answer that describes the relationship between the 2 sentences.

20. Plants need water to survive; however, some plants can live with very little water.

Cactuses, found in deserts where they don't get a lot of water, can survive with very little water.

a. The second sentence gives an example.

b. The second sentence restates an idea in the first sentence.

c. The second sentence states an effect.

d. The second sentence contrasts the first.

21. The Great Pyramids at Giza are the most famous ancient sites in Egypt.

The Great Pyramids at Giza are most often associated with Egypt and have been a main tourist attraction for hundreds of years.

a. The second sentence reinforces the first.

b. The second sentence analyzes a statement made in the first.

c. The second sentence draws a conclusion.

d. The second sentence proposes a solution.

22. Healthy people can get very sick from the flu virus and spread the virus to others.

Getting the flu vaccine is the best way to reduce the chances that you will get virus and spread it to others.

    a. The second sentence reinforces the first.

    b. The second sentence analyzes a statement made in the first.

    c. The second sentence expands on the first.

    d. The second sentence proposes a solution.

23. There is over 70% of water and less than 30% land on Earth.

Over 70% of water and less than 30% land makes up Earth.

    a. The second sentence contrasts the first.

    b. The second sentence states an effect.

    c. The second sentence restates an idea in the first sentence.

    d. The second sentence gives an example.

24. The Baltimore Ravens and the San Francisco 49ers played each other in Super Bowl XLVII.

The final score was Ravens-34 and 49ers-31, so the Ravens won the game.

    a. The second sentence reinforces the first.

    b. The second sentence analyzes a statement made in the first.

    c. The second sentence proposes a solution.

    d. The second sentence draws a conclusion.

25. The woman took her three children on an outing.

The woman took her three children on an outing to the zoo and the aquarium to see Going Bananas and Dolphin Tales, two animal shows.

    a. The second sentence reinforces the first.

    b. The second sentence analyzes a statement made in the first.

    c. The second sentence expands on the first.

    d. The second sentence proposes a solution.

26. The United States of America is the world's third largest country in terms of population.

The United States of America is one of the largest countries in terms of population.

    a. They contradict each other.

    b. They express roughly the same idea.

    c. They present problems and solutions.

    d. They establish a contrast.

27. Sophia said she is afraid of small dogs.

Sophia said she owns two teacup Yorkshire terriers.

    a. They present problems and solutions.

    b. They express roughly the same idea.

    c. They contradict each other.

    d. They establish a contrast.

28. Peggy's baby sister's, Sue, two front teeth came out.

Sue can't bite into a plum, her favorite fruit, so she cut it into bite size pieces.

    a. They express roughly the same idea.

    b. They contradict each other.

    c. They establish a contrast.

    d. They present problems and solutions.

29. An estimated 7 billion people live in the world.

There are about 7 billion people living in the world.

    a. They present problems and solutions.

    b. They contradict each other.

    c. They reinforce each other.

    d. They express roughly the same idea.

30. The cold and flu virus are both respiratory illnesses.

The common cold causes a runny nose, congestion and sore throat, but the flu virus infects the lungs, joints and intestinal tract.

    a. They repeat the same idea.

    b. They contrast each other.

    c. They reinforce each other.

    d. They provide a problem and solution.

Arithmetic

1. A map uses a scale of 1:100,000. How much distance on the ground is 3 inches on the map if the scale is in inches?

    a. 13 inches

    b. 300,000 inches

    c. 30,000 inches

    d. 333.999 inches

2. Divide 9.60 by 3.2.

    a. 2.50

    b. 3

    c. 2.3

    d. 6.4

3. Subtract 456,890 from 465,890.

    a. 9,000

    b. 7,000

    c. 8,970

    d. 8,500

4. Estimate 46,227 + 101,032.

    a. 14,700

    b. 147,000

    c. 14,700,000

    d. 104,700

5. Find the square of 25/9

a. 5/3

b. 3/5

c. 7 58/81

d. 15/2

6. Which one of the following is less than a third?

a. 84/231

b. 6/35

c. 3/22

d. b and c

7. Which of the following numbers is the largest?

a. 1

b. √2

c. 3/2ℓ

d. 4/3

8. 15/16 x 8/9 =

a. 5/6

b. 16/37

c. 2/11

d. 5/7

9. Driver B drove his car 20 km/h faster than the driver A, and driver B travelled 480 km 2 hours before driver A. What was the speed of driver A?

a. 70

b. 80

c. 60

d. 90

10. If a train travels at 72 kilometers per hour, how far will it travel in 12 seconds?

    a. 200 meters

    b. 220 meters

    c. 240 meters

    d. 260 meters

11. Tony bought 15 dozen eggs for $80. 16 eggs were broken during loading and unloading. He sold the remaining eggs for $0.54 each. What is his percent profit?

    a. 11%

    b. 11.2%

    c. 11.5%

    d. 12%

12. In a class of 83 students, 72 are present. What percent of students are absent?

    a. 12%

    b. 13%

    c. 14%

    d. 15%

13. In a local election at polling station A, 945 voters cast their vote out of 1270 registered voters. At polling station B, 860 cast their vote out of 1050 registered voters and at station C, 1210 cast their vote out of 1440 registered voters. What was the total turnout including all three polling stations?

    a. 70%

    b. 74%

    c. 76%

    d. 80%

14. Estimate 5205 ÷ 25

    a. 108

    b. 308

    c. 208

    d. 408

15. 7/15 – 3/10 =

    a. 1/6

    b. 4/5

    c. 1/7

    d. 1 1/3

16. Susan wants to buy a leather jacket that costs $545.00 and is on sale for 10% off. What is the approximate cost?

    a. $525

    b. $450

    c. $475

    d. $500

17. 11/20 ÷ 9/20 =

    a. 99/20

    b. 4 19/20

    c. 1 2/9

    d. 1 1/9

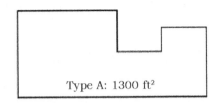

Type A: 1300 ft²

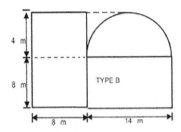

Note: Figure not drawn to scale

18. The price of houses in a certain subdivision is based on the total area. Susan is watching her budget and wants to choose the house with the lowest area. Which house type, A (1300 ft²) or B, should she choose if she would like the house with the lowest price?
(1cm² = 4.0ft² & π = 22/7)

    a. Type B is smaller 140 ft²

    b. Type A is smaller

    c. Type B is smaller at 855 ft²

    d. Type B is larger

19. Estimate 2009 x 108.

    a. 110,000

    b. 2,0000

    c. 21,000

    d. 210,000

20. Simplify 0.12 + 1 2/5 – 1 3/5

    a. 1 1/25

    b. 1 3/25

    c. 1 2/5

    d. 2 3/5

Algebra

21. Using the quadratic formula, solve the quadratic equation: $0.9x^2 + 1.8x - 2.7 = 0$

    a. 1 and 3

    b. -3 and 1

    c. -3 and -1

    d. -1 and 3

22. Subtract polynomial $5x^3 + x^2 + x + 5$ from $4x^3 - 2x^2 - 10$.

    a. $-x^3 - 3x^2 - x - 15$

    b. $9x^3 - 3x^2 - x - 15$

    c. $-x^3 - x^2 + x - 5$

    d. $9x^3 - x^2 + x + 5$

23. Find x and y from the following system of equations:

(4x + 5y)/3 = ((x - 3y)/2) + 4
(3x + y)/2 = ((2x + 7y)/3) -1

    a. (1, 3)

    b. (2, 1)

    c. (1, 1)

    d. (0, 1)

24. Using the factoring method, solve the quadratic equation: $x^2 + 12x - 13 = 0$

    a. -13 and 1

    b. -13 and -1

    c. 1 and 13

    d. -1 and 13

25. Using the quadratic formula, solve the quadratic equation: $((x^2 + 4x + 4) + (x^2 - 4x + 4)) / (x^2 - 4) = 0$.

    a. It has infinite numbers of solutions

    b. 0 and 1

    c. It has no solutions

    d. 0

26. Turn the following expression into a simple polynomial:

$5(3x^2 - 2) - x^2(2 - 3x)$

    a. $3x^3 + 17x^2 - 10$

    b. $3x^3 + 13x^2 + 10$

    c. $-3x^3 - 13x^2 - 10$

    d. $3x^3 + 13x^2 - 10$

27. Solve $(x^3 + 2)(x^2 - x) - x^5$.

    a. $2x^5 - x^4 + 2x^2 - 2x$

    b. $-x^4 + 2x^2 - 2x$

    c. $-x^4 - 2x^2 - 2x$

    d. $-x^4 + 2x^2 + 2x$

28. $9ab^2 + 8ab^2 =$

     a. ab^2

     b. $17ab^2$

     c. 17

     d. $17a^2b^2$

29. Factor the polynomial $x^2 - 7x - 30$.

     a. $(x + 15)(x - 2)$

     b. $(x + 10)(x - 3)$

     c. $(x - 10)(x + 3)$

     d. $(x - 15)(x + 2)$

30. If a and b are real numbers, solve the following equation: $(a + 2)x - b = -2 + (a + b)x$

     a. -1

     b. 0

     c. 1

     d. 2

31. If $A = -2x^4 + x^2 - 3x$, $B = x^4 - x^3 + 5$ and $C = x^4 + 2x^3 + 4x + 5$, find $A + B - C$.

     a. $x^3 + x^2 + x + 10$

     b. $-3x^3 + x^2 - 7x + 10$

     c. $-2x^4 - 3x^3 + x^2 - 7x$

     d. $-3x^4 + x^3 + x^2 - 7x$

32. $(4Y^3 - 2Y^2) + (7Y^2 + 3y - y) =$

     a. $4y^3 + 9y^2 + 4y$

     b. $5y^3 + 5y^2 + 3y$

     c. $4y^3 + 7y^2 + 2y$

     d. $4y^3 + 5y^2 + 2y$

33. Turn the following expression into a simple polynomial: 1 - x(1 - x(1 - x))

   a. $x^3 + x^2 - x + 1$

   b. $-x^3 - x^2 + x + 1$

   c. $-x^3 + x^2 - x + 1$

   d. $x^3 + x^2 - x - 1$

34. 7(2y + 8) + 1 – 4(y + 5) =

   a. $10y + 36$

   b. $10y + 77$

   c. $18y + 37$

   d. $10y + 37$

35. Richard gives 's' amount of salary to each of his 'n' employees weekly. If he has 'x' amount of money then how many days he can employ these 'n' employees.

   a. sx/7n

   b. 7x/nx

   c. nx/7s

   d. 7x/ns

36. Factor the polynomial $x^2 - 3x - 4$.

   a. $(x + 1)(x - 4)$

   b. $(x - 1)(x + 4)$

   c. $(x - 1)(x - 4)$

   d. $(x + 1)(x + 4)$

37. Solve the inequality: (2x + 1)/(2x - 1) < 1.

    a. $(-2, +\infty)$

    b. $(1, +\infty)$

    c. $(-\infty, -2)$

    d. $(-\infty, 1/2)$

38. Using the quadratic formula, solve the quadratic equation:

$(a^2 - b^2)x^2 + 2ax + 1 = 0$

    a. $a/(a + b)$ and $b/(a + b)$

    b. $1/(a + b)$ and $a/(a + b)$

    c. $a/(a + b)$ and $a/(a - b)$

    d. $-1/(a + b)$ and $-1/(a - b)$

39. Turn the following expression into a simple polynomial: (a + b) (x + y) + (a - b) (x - y) - (ax + by)

    a. $ax + by$

    b. $ax - by$

    c. $ax^2 + by^2$

    d. $ax^2 - by^2$

40. Given polynomials A = 4x⁵ - 2x² + 3x - 2 and B = -3x⁴ - 5x² -4x + 5, find A + B.

    a. $x^5 - 3x^2 - x - 3$

    b. $4x^5 - 3x^4 + 7x^2 + x + 3$

    c. $4x^5 - 3x^4 - 7x^2 - x + 3$

    d. $4x^5 - 3x^4 - 7x^2 - x - 7$

College Level

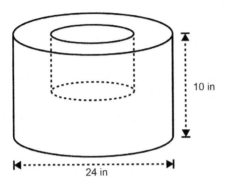

10 in

24 in

Note: Figure not drawn to scale

41. What is the volume of the above solid made by a hollow cylinder that is half the size (in all dimensions) of the larger cylinder?

    a. 1440 π in³

    b. 1260 π in³

    c. 1040 π in³

    d. 960 π in³

42. Find x if $\log_{1/2} x = 4$.

    a. 16

    b. 8

    c. 1/8

    d. 1/16

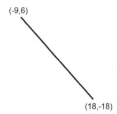

43. What is the slope of the line above?

    a. -8/9
    b. 9/8
    c. -9/8
    d. 8/9

44. If the sequence $\{a_n\}$ is defined by $a_{n+1} = 1 - a_n$ and $a_2 = 6$, find a_4.

    a. 2
    b. 1
    c. 6
    d. -1

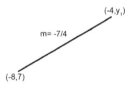

45. With the data given above, what is the value of y_1?

    a. 0
    b. -7
    c. 7
    d. 8

46. The area of a rectangle is 20 cm². If one side increases by 1 cm and other by 2 cm, the area of the new rectangle is 35 cm². Find the sides of the original rectangle.

> a. (4,8)
>
> b. (4,5)
>
> c. (2.5,8)
>
> d. b and c

47. Solve $\log_{10} 10,000 = x$.

> a. 2
>
> b. 4
>
> c. 3
>
> d. 6

(18,12)

(9,-6)

48. What is the distance between the two points?

> a. ≈ 19
>
> b. 20
>
> c. ≈ 21
>
> d. ≈ 22

49. If in the right triangle, a is 12 and sinα=12/13, find cosα.

    a. -5/13

    b. -1/13

    c. 1/13

    d. 5/13

50. Find the solution for the following linear equation: 1/(4x - 2) = 5/6

    a. 0.2

    b. 0.4

    c. 0.6

    d. 0.8

(-1,2)

(-4,-4)

51. What is the slope of the line above?

    a. 1

    b. 2

    c. 3

    d. -2

52. How much water can be stored in a cylindrical container 5 meters in diameter and 12 meters high?

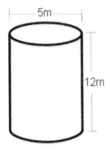

a. 235.65 m³

b. 223.65 m³

c. 240.65 m³

d. 252.65 m³

53. If members of the sequence {an} are represented by $a_{n+1} = - a_{n-1}$ and $a_2 = 3$ and, find $a_3 + a_4$.

a. 2

b. 3

c. 0

d. -2

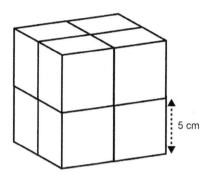

Note: Figure not drawn to scale

54. Assuming the figure above is composed of cubes, what is the volume?

     a. 125 cm^3

     b. 875 cm^3

     c. 1000 cm^3

     d. 500 cm^3

55. Solve

$$x \sqrt{5} - y = \sqrt{5}$$
$$x - y \sqrt{5} = 5$$

     a. $(0, -\sqrt{5})$

     b. $(0, \sqrt{5})$

     c. $(-\sqrt{5}, 0)$

     d. $(\sqrt{5}, 0)$

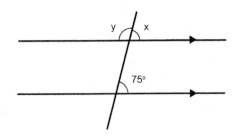

56. What is the value of the angle y?

    a. 25°

    b. 15°

    c. 30°

    d. 105°

57. Using the right triangle's legs, calculate (sinα + cosβ)/(tgα + ctgβ).

    a. a/b

    b. b/c

    c. b/a

    d. a/c

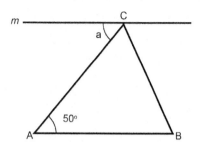

58. If the line *m* is parallel to the side AB of △ABC, what is angle *a*?

    a. 130°

    b. 25°

    c. 65°

    d. 50°

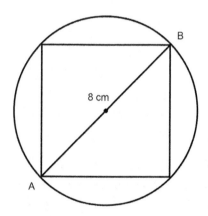

Note: figure not drawn to scale

59. What is area of the circle above?

    a. $4 \pi \ cm^2$

    b. $12 \pi \ cm^2$

    c. $10 \pi \ cm^2$

    d. $16 \pi \ cm^2$

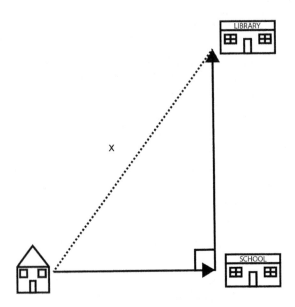

Note: figure not drawn to scale

60. Every day starting from his home Peter travels due east 3 kilometers to the school. After school he travels due north 4 kilometers to the library. What is the distance between Peter's home and the library?

    a. 15 km

    b. 10 km

    c. 5 km

    d. 12 ½ km

Sentence Skills

Directions: Select the best version of the underlined portion of the sentence

1. <u>Who</u> won first place in the Western Division?

    a. Whom won first place in the Western Division?

    b. Which won first place in the Western Division?

    c. What won first place in the Western Division?

    d. No change is necessary?

2. There are now several ways to listen to music, including radio, CDs, and Mp3 files <u>which</u> you can download onto an MP3 player.

    a. There are now several ways to listen to music, including radio, CDs, and Mp3 files on which you can download onto an MP3 player.

    b. There are now several ways to listen to music, including radio, CDs, and Mp3 files who you can download onto an MP3 player.

    c. There are now several ways to listen to music, including radio, CDs, and Mp3 files whom you can download onto an MP3 player.

    d. No change is necessary.

3. As the tallest monument in the United States, the St. Louis Arch <u>was rose to an impressive 630 feet</u>.

    a. As the tallest monument in the United States, the St. Louis Arch has rose to an impressive 630 feet.

    b. As the tallest monument in the United States, the St. Louis Arch is risen to an impressive 630 feet.

    c. As the tallest monument in the United States, the St. Louis Arch rises to an impressive 630 feet.

    d. No change is necessary.

4. The tired, old woman should <u>lain</u> on the sofa.

    a. The tired, old woman should lie on the sofa.

    b. The tired, old woman should lays on the sofa.

    c. The tired, old woman should laid on the sofa.

    d. No changes are necessary.

5. Did the students understand that Thanksgiving always <u>fallen</u> on the fourth Thursday in November?

    a No change is necessary.

    b. Did the students understand that Thanksgiving always falling on the fourth Thursday in November.

    c. Did the students understand that Thanksgiving always has fell on the fourth Thursday in November.

    d. Did the students understand that Thanksgiving always falls on the fourth Thursday in November.

6. Collecting stamps, <u>build models</u>, and listening to shortwave radio were Rick's main hobbies.

    a. Collecting stamps, building models, and listening to shortwave radio were Rick's main hobbies.

    b. Collecting stamps, to build models, and listening to shortwave radio were Rick's main hobbies.

    c. Collecting stamps, having built models, and listening to shortwave radio were Rick's main hobbies.

    d. No change is necessary.

7. This morning, <u>after the kids will leave for school</u> and before the sun came up, my mother makes herself a cup of cocoa.

a. This morning, after the kids had left for school and before the sun came up, my mother makes herself a cup of cocoa.

b. This morning, after the kids leave for school and before the sun came up, my mother makes herself a cup of cocoa.

c. This morning, after the kids have left for school and before the sun came up, my mother makes herself a cup of cocoa.

d. No change is necessary.

8. Elaine promised to bring the camera <u>to me</u> at the mall yesterday.

a. Elaine promised to bring the camera by me at the mall yesterday.

b. Elaine promised to bring the camera with me at the mall yesterday.

c. Elaine promised to bring the camera at me at the mall yesterday.

d. No changes are necessary.

9. Last night, he <u>laid</u> the sleeping bag down beside my mattress.

a. Last night, he lay the sleeping bag down beside my mattress.

b. Last night, he lain

c. Last night, he has laid

d. No change is necessary.

10. I would have bought the shirt for you <u>if I know</u> you liked it.

    a. I would have bought the shirt for you if I had known you liked it.

    b. I would have bought the shirt for you if I have known you liked it.

    c. I would have bought the shirt for you if I would know you liked it.

    d. No change is necessary.

For questions 11 - 20, rewrite the sentence given keeping the same meaning.

11. Though less spectacular, lunar eclipses occur more frequently than the solar ones.

Rewrite, beginning with

Lunar eclipses occur more frequently than the solar ones,

The next words will be

    a. and they are less spectacular

    b. though less spectacular

    c. but they are less spectacular

    d. but it is less spectacular

12. It is unwise to drink too many cups of coffee, but green tea is always a healthy option.

Rewrite, beginning with

Unlike coffee,

The next words will be

> a. it is always healthy to
>
> b. you can always drink
>
> c. green tea is always
>
> d. it is unwise to

13. Shark teeth are very sharp, but they fall out easily.

Rewrite, beginning with

Even though they are very sharp,

The next words will be

> a. shark teeth fall out
>
> b. falling out easily
>
> c. but shark teeth fall out
>
> d. it is easy that

14. Missing their two best players, the team will not be able to score as easily.

Rewrite, beginning with

It is not as easy for the team to score

The next words will be

> a. without their two best
>
> b. and their two best
>
> c. being absent their two best
>
> d. but since their two best

15. Antoine ate the appetizer and then went on to the main course.

Rewrite, beginning with

Before going on to the main course,

The next words will be

> a. Antoine ate
>
> b. eating first the main
>
> c. and then Antoine
>
> d. it was the main course

16. Skating along the boardwalk, Kathy spotted her friend in the surf.

Rewrite, beginning with

Kathy spotted her friend in the surf

The next words will be

     a. after skating along the

     b. and then skated along the

     c. along the boardwalk

     d. as she was skating along the

17. As omnivores, bears eat berries and other animals.

Rewrite, beginning with

Eating berries and other animals,

The next words will be

     a. because omnivores

     b. bears are omnivores

     c. although omnivores

     d. bears are omnivores

18. Volcanoes hardly ever erupt, and even more rarely do they endanger human life.

Rewrite, beginning with

Volcanoes endanger human life even more rarely

The next words will be

    a. and erupt

    b. than they erupt

    c. although erupting

    d. but then they erupt

19. Not having studied until the morning of the test, Jeremy was tired and anxious as he wrote down his answers.

Rewrite, beginning with

Jeremy was tired and anxious as he wrote down his answers

The next words will be

    a. although he had not studied

    b. not having studied

    c. because he had not studied

    d. until the morning of the test

20. Claire enjoyed the film, but she wished it had ended more happily.

Rewrite, beginning with

Wishing it had ended more happily,

The next words will be

      a. Claire nonetheless enjoyed

      b. Claire enjoyed

      c. the film was nonetheless enjoyed

      d. although enjoying the film

Answer Key

Reading Comprehension

1. A
Secede most nearly means to break away from because the 11 states wanted to leave the United States and form their own country.

Option B is incorrect because the states were not accomplishing anything. Option C is incorrect because the states were trying to leave the USA not join it. Option D is incorrect because the states seceded before they lost the war.

2. B
Look at the dates in the passage. The shots were fired on April 12 and Congress declared war on April 14.

Option C is incorrect because the passage states that Lincoln was against slavery. Option D is incorrect because it never mentions who was or was not at Fort Sumter.

3. C
The passage states that Lee surrendered to Grant after the capture of the capital of the Confederacy, which is Richmond.

Option A is incorrect because the war continued for 2 years after Gettysburg. Option B is incorrect because that battle is not mentioned in the passage. Option D is incorrect because the capture of the capital occurred after the march to the sea.

4. A
When the passage said that the North had *abolished* slavery, it implies that slaves were no longer allowed in the North. In essence slavery was banned.

Option B makes no sense relative to the context of the passage. Option C is incorrect because we know the North was fighting against slavery, not for it. Option D is incorrect because slavery is not a tangible thing that can be destroyed. It is a practice that had to be outlawed or banned.

5. A
We can infer that, an electrical discharge in the clouds causes lightning.

The passage tells us that, "Lightning occurs when static electricity inside clouds builds up and causes an electrical charge,"

6. C
Being struck by lightning means, a ninety percent chance of surviving the strike.

From the passage, "statistics show that 90% of victims survive a lightning blast."

7. A
We know that lightning is static electricity from the third sentence in the passage. We also know that water droplets colliding with ice crystals cause static electricity. Therefore, Lightning is caused by water droplets colliding with ice crystals.

8. A
Low blood sugar occurs both in diabetics and healthy adults.

9. B
None of the statements are the author's opinion.

10. A
The author's purpose is the inform.

11. A
The only statement that is not a detail is, "A doctor can diagnosis this medical condition by asking the patient questions and testing."

12. B
This passage describes the different categories for traditional stories. The other choices are facts from the passage, not the main idea of the passage. The main idea of a passage will

always be the most general statement. For example, Choice A, Myths, fables, and folktales are not the same thing, and each describes a specific type of story. This is a true statement from the passage, but not the main idea of the passage, since the passage also talks about how some cultures may classify a story as a myth and others as a folktale. The statement, from choice B, Traditional stories can be categorized in different ways by different people, is a more general statement that describes the passage.

13. B
Choice B is the best choice, categories that group traditional stories according to certain characteristics.

Choices A and C are false and can be eliminated right away. Choice D is designed to confuse. Choice D may be true, but it is not mentioned in the passage.

14. D
The best answer is D, traditional stories themselves are a part of the larger category of folklore, which may also include costumes, gestures, and music.

All the other choices are false. Traditional stories are part of the larger category of Folklore, which includes other things, not the other way around.

15. A
The sentence is a recommendation.

16. C
Tips for a good night's sleep is the best alternative title for this article.

17. B
Mental activity is helpful for a good night's sleep is can not be inferred from this article.

18. C
This question tests the reader's vocabulary and contextualization skills. A may or may not be true, but focuses on the wrong function of the word "give" and ignores the rest of the sentence, which is more relevant to what the passage is discussing. B and D may also be selected if the reader depends

too literally on the word "give," failing to grasp the more abstract function of the word that is the focus of answer C, which also properly acknowledges the entirety of the passage and its meaning.

19. A
Navy Seals are the maritime component of the United States Special Operations Command (USSOCOM).

20. A
Plants need water to survive; however, some plants can live with very little water.

Cactuses, found in deserts where they don't get a lot of water, can survive with very little water.

The second sentence gives an example of a plant that can live with very little water.

21. A
The Great Pyramids at Giza are the most famous ancient sites in Egypt.

The Great Pyramids at Giza are most often associated with Egypt and have been a main tourist attraction for hundreds of years.

The second sentence reinforces the first with supporting details.

22. D
Healthy people can get very sick from the flu virus and spread the virus to others.

Getting the flu vaccine is the best way to reduce the chances that you will get virus and spread it to others.

The second sentence proposes a solution for the problem mentioned in the first sentence.

23. C
There is over 70% of water and less than 30% land on Earth.

Over 70% of water and less than 30% land makes up Earth.

The second sentence restates an idea in the first sentence.

24. D
The Baltimore Ravens and the San Francisco 49ers played each other in Super Bowl XLVII.

The score was Ravens-34 and 49ers-31.

The second sentence reveals the outcome (results) of the game.

25. C
The woman took her three children on an outing.

The woman took her three children on an outing to the zoo and the aquarium to see Going Bananas and Dolphin Tales, two animal shows.

The second sentence expands on the first sentence because it expresses in greater detail where the mother took her children.

26. B
The United States of America is the world's third largest country in terms of population.

The United States of America is one of the largest countries in terms of population.

The second sentence expresses roughly the same idea.

27. C
Sophia said she is afraid of small dogs.

Sophia said she owns two teacup Yorkshire terriers.

The two sentences contradict each other.

28. D
Peggy's baby sister's, Sue, two front teeth came out.

Sue can't bite into a plum, her favorite fruit, so she cut it into bite size pieces.

The second sentence provides a problem and solution.

29. D
An estimated 7 billion people live in the world.

There are about 7 billion people living in the world.

The second sentence expresses roughly the same idea.

30. B
The cold and flu virus are both respiratory illnesses.

The common cold causes a runny nose, congestion and sore throat, but the flu virus infects the lungs, joints and intestinal tract.

They contrast each other.

The second sentence describes the differences between the cold and flu virus whereas the first compares their similarities.

Arithmetic

1. B
1 inch on map = 100,000 inches on ground. So 3 inches on map = 3 x 100,000 = 300,000 inches on ground.

2. B
9.60/3.2 = 3

3. A
465,890 - 456,890 = 9,000.

4. B
46,227 + 101,032 is about 147,000. The exact answer is 147,259.

5. C
$(25/9)^2 = 625/81$

6. D
$84/231 = 12/33 > 1/3$
$6/35 = 1/5 < 1/3$
$3/22 = 1/7 < 1/3$

7. B
$\sqrt{2}$ is the largest number.
Here are the choices:

    a. 1

    b. $\sqrt{2} = 1.414$

    c. $3/22 = .1563$

    d. $4/3 = 1.33$

8. A
First cancel out 15/16 x 8/9 to get 5/2 x 1/3, then multiply numerators and denominators to get 5/6.

9. B
We are told that driver B is 20 km/h faster than driver A. So:
$V_B = V_A + 20$ where V is the velocity. Also, driver B travelled 480 km 2 hours before driver A. So:

$x = 480$ km

$t_A - 2 = t_B$ where t is the time. Now we know the relationship between A and B drivers in terms of time and velocity. We need to write an equation only depending on V_A (the speed of driver A) which we are asked to find.

Since distance = velocity•time: $480 = V_A \cdot t_A = V_B \cdot t_B$

$480 = (V_A + 20)(t_A - 2)$

$480 = (V_A + 20)(480/V_A - 2)$

$480 = 480 - 2V_A + 20 \cdot 480/V_A - 40$

$0 = -2V_A + 9600/V_A - 40$ ... Multiplying the equation by V_A eliminates the denominator:

$2V_A^2 + 40V_A - 9600 = 0$ ... Simplifying the equation by 2:

$V_A^2 + 20V_A - 4800 = 0$

$V_{A1,2} = [-20 \pm \sqrt{(400 + 4 \cdot 4800)}] / 2$

$V_{A1,2} = [-20 \pm 140] / 2$

$V_A = [-20 - 140]/2 = -80$ km/h and $V_A = [-20 + 140]/2 = 60$ km/h

We need to check our answers. It is easy to make a table:

t_A	V_A	V_B	t_B	$t_A - t_B$
480/80 = 6	-80	-80 - 20 = -100 B is 20 km/h faster than A. - sign only mentions the direction of the velocity. For magnitude, we need to add -20.	480/100 = 4.8	6 - 4.8 = 1.2 This should be 2!
480/60 = 8	60	60 + 20 = 80	480/80 = 6	8 - 6 = 2 This is correct !

So, $V_A = 60$ km/h is the only answer satisfying the question.

10. C
1 hour is equal to 3,600 seconds and 1 kilometer is equal to 1000 meters.

Since this train travels 72 kilometers per hour, this means that it covers 72,000 meters in 3,600 seconds.

If it travels 72,000 meters in 3,600 seconds

It travels x meters in 12 seconds

By cross multiplication: x = 72,000 • 12 / 3,600

x = 240 meters

11. A
Let us first mention the money Tony spent: $80

Now we need to find the money Tony earned:

He had 15 dozen eggs = 15•12 = 180 eggs. 16 eggs were broken. So,

Remaining number of eggs that Tony sold = 180 – 16 = 164.

Total amount he earned for selling 164 eggs = 164•0.54 = $88.56.

As a summary, he spent $80 and earned $88.56.

The profit is the difference: 88.56 - 80 = $8.56

Percentage profit is found by proportioning the profit to the money he spent:

8.56•100/80 = 10.7%

Checking the answers, we round 10.7 to the nearest whole number: 11%

12. B
Number of absent students = 83 – 72 = 11

Percentage of absent students is found by proportioning the number of absent students to total number of students in the class = 11•100/83 = 13.25

Checking the answers, we round 13.25 to the nearest whole number: 13%

13. D
To find the total turnout in all three polling stations, we need to proportion the number of voters to the number of all registered voters.

Number of total voters = 945 + 860 + 1210 = 3015

Number of total registered voters = 1270 + 1050 + 1440 = 3760

Percentage turnout over all three polling stations = 3015•100/3760 = 80.19%

Checking the answers, we round 80.19 to the nearest whole number: 80%

14. C
The approximate answer to 5205 ÷ 25 is 208. The exact answer is 208.2.

15. A
A common denominator is needed, a number which both 15 and 10 will divide into. So 14-9/30 = 5/30 = 1/6

16. D
The jacket costs $545.00 so we can round up to $550. 10% of $550 is 55. We can round down to $50, which is easier to work with. $550 - $50 is $500. The jacket will cost about $500.

The actual cost is 545 - 54.50 = 490.50.

17. C X $\mathcal{D}$
11/20 x 20/9 = 11/1 x 1/9 = 11/9 = 1 2/9

18. C
Area of Type B consists of two rectangles and a half circle. We can find these three areas and sum them up in order to find the total area:

Area of the left rectangle: $(4 + 8) \cdot 8 = 96$ m^2

Area of the right rectangle: $14 \cdot 8 = 112$ m^2

The diameter of the circle is equal to 14 m. So, the radius is 14/2 = 7:

Area of the half circle = $(1/2) \cdot \pi r^2 = (1/2) \cdot (22/7) \cdot (7)^2 = (1 \cdot 22 \cdot 49)/(2 \cdot 7) = 77$ m^2

Area of Type B = 96 + 112 + 77 = 285 m^2

Converting this area to ft^2: 285 m^2 = $285 \cdot 10.76$ ft^2 = 3066.6 ft^2

Type B is (3066.6 - 1300 = 1766.6 ft^2) 1766.6 ft^2 larger than type A.

19. D
2009 x 108 is about 210,000. The exact answer is 216,972.

20. B
0.12 + 2/5 + 3/5, Convert decimal to fraction to get 3/25 + 2/5 + 3/5, = (3 + 10 + 15)/25, = 28/25 = 1 3/25

Algebra

21. B
To solve the equation, we need the equation in the form $ax^2 + bx + c = 0$.
$0.9x^2 + 1.8x - 2.7 = 0$ is already in this form.

The quadratic formula to find the roots of a quadratic equation is:

$x_{1,2} = (-b \pm \sqrt{\Delta}) / 2a$ where $\Delta = b^2 - 4ac$ and is called the discriminant of the quadratic equation.

In our question, the equation is $0.9x^2 + 1.8x - 2.7 = 0$. To eliminate the decimals, let us multiply the equation by 10:

$9x^2 + 18x - 27 = 0$ ... This equation can be simplified by 9 since each term contains 9:

$x^2 + 2x - 3 = 0$

By remembering the form $ax^2 + bx + c = 0$:

$a = 1, b = 2, c = -3$

So, we can find the discriminant first, and then the roots of the equation:

$\Delta = b^2 - 4ac = (2)^2 - 4 \bullet 1 \bullet (-3) = 4 + 12 = 16$

$x_{1,2} = (-b \pm \sqrt{\Delta}) / 2a = (-2 \pm \sqrt{16}) / 2 = (-2 \pm 4) / 2$

This means that the roots are,

$x_1 = (-2 - 4)/2 = -3$ and $x_2 = (-2 + 4)/2 = 1$

22. A
We are asked to subtract polynomials. By paying attention to the sign distribution; we write the polynomials and operate:

$4x^3 - 2x^2 - 10 - (5x^3 + x^2 + x + 5) = 4x^3 - 2x^2 - 10 - 5x^3 - x^2 - x - 5$

$= 4x^3 - 5x^3 - 2x^2 - x^2 - x - 10 - 5$ ... similar terms written together to ease summing/substituting.

$= -x^3 - 3x^2 - x - 15$

23. C

First, we need to arrange the two equations to obtain the form ax + by = c. We see that there are 3 and 2 in the denominators of both equations. If we equate all at 6, then we can cancel all 6 in the denominators and have straight equations:

Equate all denominators at 6:

$2(4x + 5y)/6 = 3(x - 3y)/6 + 4•6/6$ ... Now we can cancel 6 in the denominators:

$8x + 10y = 3x - 9y + 24$ ... We can collect x and y terms on left side of the equation:

$8x + 10y - 3x + 9y = 24$

$5x + 19y = 24$ ... Equation (I)

Let us arrange the second equation:

$3(3x + y)/6 = 2(2x + 7y)/6 - 1•6/6$ ... Now we can cancel 6 in the denominators:

$9x + 3y = 4x + 14y - 6$ ... We can collect x and y terms on left side of the equation:

$9x + 3y - 4x - 14y = -6$

$5x - 11y = -6$ ... Equation (II)

Now, we have two equations and two unknowns x and y. By writing the two equations one under the other and operating, we can find one unknowns first, and find the other next:

$5x + 19y = 24$

$-1/ 5x - 11y = -6$ ... If we substitute this equation from the upper one, 5x cancels -5x:

$5x + 19y = 24$

$-5x + 11y = 6$ ... Summing side-by-side:

$5x - 5x + 19y + 11y = 24 + 6$

$30y = 30$ ... Dividing both sides by 30:

$y = 1$

Inserting y = 1 into either of the equations, we can find the value of x. Choosing equation I:

5x + 19•1 = 24

5x = 24 - 19

5x = 5 ... Dividing both sides by 5:

x = 1

So, x = 1 and y = 1 is the solution; it is shown as (1, 1).

24. A
x^2 + 12x - 13 = 0 ... We try to separate the middle term 12x to find common factors with x^2 and -13 separately:

x^2 + 13x - x - 13 = 0 ... Here, we see that x is a common factor for x^2 and 13x, and -1 is a common factor for -x and -13:

x(x + 13) - 1(x + 13) = 0 ... Here, we have x times x + 13 and -1 times x + 13 summed up. This means that we have x - 1 times x + 13:

(x - 1)(x + 13) = 0

This is true when either or, both of the expressions in the parenthesis are equal to zero:

x - 1 = 0 ... x = 1

x + 13 = 0 ... x = -13

1 and -13 are the solutions for this quadratic equation.

25. C
First, we need to simplify the equation:
((x^2 + 4x + 4) + (x^2 - 4x + 4)) / (x^2 - 4) = 0

(x^2 + 4x + 4 + x^2 - 4x + 4) / (x^2 - 4) = 0 ... 4x and -4x in the numerator cancel each other.

Note that x^2 - 4 is two square difference and is equal to x^2 - 2^2 = (x - 2)(x + 2):

($2x^2$ + 8)/((x - 2)(x + 2)) = 0

The denominator tells us that if x - 2 or x + 2 equals to zero, there will be no solution. So, we will need to eliminate x = 2 and x = -2 from our solution which will be found considering the numerator:

$2x^2 + 8 = 0$

$2(x^2 + 4) = 0$

$x^2 + 4 = 0$

$x^2 = -4$ ... We know that, a square cannot be equal to a negative number. Solution for the square root of -4 is not a real number, so this equation has no solution.

26. D
We need to distribute the factors to the terms inside the related parenthesis:

$5(3x^2 - 2) - x^2(2 - 3x) = 15x^2 - 10 - (2x^2 - 3x^3)$

$= 15x^2 - 10 - 2x^2 + 3x^3$

$= 3x^3 + 15x^2 - 2x^2 - 10$ ... similar terms written together to ease summing/substituting.

$= 3x^3 + 13x^2 - 10$

27. B
We need to distribute the factors to the terms inside the related parenthesis:

$(x^3 + 2)(x^2 - x) - x^5 = x^5 - x^4 + (2x^2 - 2x) - x^5$

$= x^5 - x^4 + 2x^2 - 2x - x^5$

$= x^5 - x^5 - x^4 + 2x^2 - 2x$ ... similar terms written together to ease summing/substituting.

$= -x^4 + 2x^2 - 2x$

28. B
To simplify the expression, we need to find common factors. We see that both terms contain the term ab^2. So, we can take this term out of each term as a factor:

$9ab^2 + 8ab^2 = (9 + 8)\,ab^2 = 17ab^2$

29. C

$x^2 - 7x - 30 = 0$ ... We try to separate the middle term -7x to find common factors with x^2 and -30 separately:

$x^2 - 10x + 3x - 30 = 0$ ... Here, we see that x is a common factor for x^2 and -10x, and 3 is a common factor for 3x and -30:

$x(x - 10) + 3(x - 10) = 0$ ... Here, we have x times x - 10 and 3 times x - 10 summed up. This means that we have x + 3 times x - 10:

$(x + 3)(x - 10) = 0$ or $(x - 10)(x + 3) = 0$

30. A

We need to simplify the equation by distributing factors and then collecting x terms on one side, and the others on the other side:

$(a + 2)x - b = -2 + (a + b)x$

$ax + 2x - b = -2 + ax + bx$

$ax + 2x - ax - bx = -2 + b$ ... ax and -ax cancel each other:

$2x - bx = -2 + b$ ... we take -1 as a factor on the right side:

$(2 - b)x = -(2 - b)$

$x = -(2 - b)/(2 - b)$ ... Simplifying by 2 - b:

$x = -1$

31. C

We are asked to find A + B - C. By paying attention to the sign distribution; we write the polynomials and operate:

$A + B - C = (-2x^4 + x^2 - 3x) + (x^4 - x^3 + 5) - (x^4 + 2x^3 + 4x + 5)$

$= -2x^4 + x^2 - 3x + x^4 - x^3 + 5 - x^4 - 2x^3 - 4x - 5$

$= -2x^4 + x^4 - x^4 - x^3 - 2x^3 + x^2 - 3x - 4x + 5 - 5$ ... similar terms written together to ease summing/substituting.

$= -2x^4 - 3x^3 + x^2 - 7x$

32. D
To simplify, we remove parenthesis:

$(4y^3 - 2y^2) + (7y^2 + 3y - y) = 4y^3 - 2y^2 + 7y^2 + 3y - y$ ... Then, we operate within similar terms:

$= 4y^3 + (-2 + 7)y^2 + (3 - 1)y = 4y^3 + 5y^2 + 2y$

33. C
To obtain a polynomial, we should remove the parenthesis by distributing the related factors to the terms inside the parenthesis:
$1 - x(1 - x(1 - x)) = 1 - x(1 - (x - x \cdot x)) = 1 - x(1 - x + x^2)$

$= 1 - (x - x \cdot x + x \cdot x^2) = 1 - x + x^2 - x^3$ ... Writing this result in descending order of powers:

$= -x^3 + x^2 - x + 1$

34. D
To simplify the expression, remove the parenthesis by distributing the related factors to the terms inside the parenthesis:

$7(2y + 8) + 1 - 4(y + 5) = (7 \cdot 2y + 7 \cdot 8) + 1 - (4 \cdot y + 4 \cdot 5)$

$= 14y + 56 + 1 - 4y - 20$

$= 14y - 4y + 56 + 1 - 20$ ... similar terms written together to ease summing/substituting.

$= 10y + 37$

35. D
We understand that each of the n employees earn s amount of salary weekly. This means that one employee earns s salary weekly. So; Richard has ns amount of money to employ n employees for a week.

We are asked to find the number of days n employees can be employed with x amount of money. We can do simple direct proportion:

If Richard can employ n employees for 7 days with ns amount of money,

Richard can employ n employees for y days with x amount of money ... y is the number of days we need to find.

We can do cross multiplication:

y = (x•7)/(ns)

y = 7x/ns

36. A
x^2 - 3x - 4 ... We try to separate the middle term -3x to find common factors with x^2 and -4 separately:

x^2 + x - 4x - 4 ... Here, we see that x is a common factor for x^2 and x, and -4 is a common factor for -4x and -4:

= x(x + 1) - 4(x + 1) ... Here, we have x times x + 1 and -4 times x + 1 summed up. This means that we have x - 4 times x + 1:

= (x - 4)(x + 1) or (x + 1)(x - 4)

37. D
We need to simplify and have x alone and on one side in order to solve the inequality:

(2x + 1)/(2x - 1) < 1

(2x + 1)/(2x - 1) - 1 < 0 ... We need to write the left side at the common denominator 2x - 1:

(2x + 1)/(2x - 1) - (2x - 1)/(2x - 1) < 0

(2x + 1 - 2x + 1)/(2x - 1) < 0 ... 2x and -2x terms cancel each other in the numerator:

2/(2x - 1) < 0

2 is a positive number; so,

2x - 1 < 0

2x < 1

x < 1/2 ... This means that x should be smaller than 1/2 and not equal to 1/2. This is shown as (-∞, 1/2).

38. D

To solve the equation, we need the equation in the form $ax^2 + bx + c = 0$.
$(a^2 - b^2)x^2 + 2ax + 1 = 0$ is already in this form.

The quadratic formula to find the roots of a quadratic equation is:

$x_{1,2} = (-b \pm \sqrt{\Delta}) / 2a$ where $\Delta = b^2 - 4ac$ and is called the discriminant of the quadratic equation.

In our question, the equation is $(a^2 - b^2)x^2 + 2ax + 1 = 0$.

By remembering the form $ax^2 + bx + c = 0$: $a = a^2 - b^2$, $b = 2a$, $c = 1$

So, we can find the discriminant first, and then the roots of the equation:

$\Delta = b^2 - 4ac = (2a)^2 - 4(a^2 - b^2) \cdot 1 = 4a^2 - 4a^2 + 4b^2 = 4b^2$

$x_{1,2} = (-b \pm \sqrt{\Delta}) / 2a = (-2a \pm \sqrt{4b^2}) / (2(a^2 - b^2)) = (-2a \pm 2b) / (2(a^2 - b^2))$

$= 2(-a \pm b) / (2(a^2 - b^2))$ ... We can simplify by 2:

$= (-a \pm b) / (a^2 - b^2)$

This means that the roots are,

$x_1 = (-a - b) / (a^2 - b^2)$ ... $a^2 - b^2$ is two square differences:

$x_1 = -(a + b) / ((a - b)(a + b))$ ... $(a + b)$ terms cancel each other:

$x_1 = -1/(a - b)$

$x_2 = (-a + b) / (a^2 - b^2)$ ... $a^2 - b^2$ is two square differences:

$x_2 = -(a - b) / ((a - b)(a + b))$ ... $(a - b)$ terms cancel each other:

$x_2 = -1/(a + b)$

39. A

To simplify, we need to remove the parenthesis and see if any terms cancel:

(a + b)(x + y) + (a - b)(x - y) - (ax + by) = ax + ay + bx + by + ax - ay - bx + by - ax - by

By writing similar terms together:

= ax + ax - ax + bx - bx + ay - ay + by + by - by ... + terms cancel - terms:

= ax + by

40. C
We are asked to add polynomials A + B. By paying attention to the sign distribution; we write the polynomials and operate:

A + B = $(4x^5 - 2x^2 + 3x - 2) + (-3x^4 - 5x^2 - 4x + 5)$

= $4x^5 - 2x^2 + 3x - 2 - 3x^4 - 5x^2 - 4x + 5$ ... Writing similar terms together:

= $4x^5 - 3x^4 - 2x^2 - 5x^2 + 3x - 4x - 2 + 5$ ... Operating within similar terms:

= $4x^5 - 3x^4 - 7x^2 - x + 3$

College Level

41. B
Total Volume = Volume of large cylinder - Volume of small cylinder

Volume of a cylinder = area of base • height = $\pi r^2 \cdot h$

Total Volume = $(\pi \cdot 12^2 \cdot 10) - (\pi \cdot 6^2 \cdot 5) = 1440\pi - 180\pi$

= 1260π in^3

42. D
$\log_{1/2} x = 4$ ... We know that $\log_a a^b = b \cdot \log_a a = b \cdot 1 = b$
$\log_{1/2} x = \log_{1/2}(1/2)^4$ ... Now, we can remove $\log_{1/2}$ terms since both sides have this function applied:

x = $(1/2)^4$

x = $1^4/2^4$

x = 1/16

43. A
If we know the coordinates of two points on a line, we can find the slope (m) with the below formula:

m = $(y_2 - y_1)/(x_2 - x_1)$ where (x_1, y_1) represent the coordinates of one point and (x_2, y_2) the other.

In this question:

(-9, 6) : x_1 = -9, y_1 = 6

(18, -18) : x_2 = 18, y_2 = -18

Inserting these values into the formula:

m = (-18 - 6)/(18 - (-9)) = (-24)/(27) ... Simplifying by 3:

m = -8/9

44. C
We are given that,
a_2 = 6

a_{n+1} = 1 - a_n

Starting from the second term, we can reach the fourth term:

n = 2 ... a_3 = 1 - a_2 = 1 - 6 = -5

n = 3 ... a_4 = 1 - a_3 = 1 - (-5) = 1 + 5 = 6

45. A
If we know the coordinates of two points on a line, we can find the slope (m) with the below formula:
m = $(y_2 - y_1)/(x_2 - x_1)$ where (x_1, y_1) represent the coordinates of one point and (x_2, y_2) the other.

In this question:

(-4, y_1) : x_1 = -4, y_1 = we will find

(-8, 7) : x_2 = -8, y_2 = 7

m = -7/4

Inserting these values into the formula:

-7/4 = (7 - y_1)/(-8 - (-4))

-7/4 = (7 - y_1)/(-8 + 4)

7/(-4) = (7 - y_1)/(-4) ... Simplifying the denominators of both sides by -4:

7 = 7 - y_1

0 = -y_1

y_1 = 0

46. D

The area of a rectangle is found by multiplying the width to the length. If we call these sides with "a" and "b"; the area is = a•b.

We are given that a•b = 20 cm² ... Equation I

One side is increased by 1 and the other by 2 cm. So new side lengths are "a + 1" and "b + 2".

The new area is (a + 1)(b + 2) = 35 cm² ... Equation II

Using equations I and II, we can find a and b:

ab = 20

(a + 1)(b + 2) = 35 ... We need to distribute the terms in parenthesis:

ab + 2a + b + 2 = 35

We can insert ab = 20 to the above equation:

20 + 2a + b + 2 = 35

2a + b = 35 - 2 - 20

2a + b = 13 ... This is one equation with two unknowns. We need to use another information to have two equations with two unknowns which leads us to the solution. We know that ab = 20. So, we can use a = 20/b:

2(20/b) + b = 13

40/b + b = 13 ... We equate all denominators to "b" and eliminate it:

$40 + b^2 = 13b$

$b2 - 13b + 40 = 0$ ... We can use the roots by factoring. We try to separate the middle term -13b to find common factors with b2 and 40 separately:

$b2 - 8b - 5b + 40 = 0$ ... Here, we see that b is a common factor for b2 and -8b, and -5 is a common factor for -5b and 40:

$b(b - 8) - 5(b - 8) = 0$ Here, we have b times b - 8 and -5 times b - 8 summed up. This means that we have b - 5 times b - 8:

$(b - 5)(b - 8) = 0$

This is true when either or both of the expressions in the parenthesis are equal to zero:

$b - 5 = 0$ ... $b = 5$

$b - 8 = 0$ ... $b = 8$

So we have two values for b which means we have two values for a as well. In order to find a, we can use any equation we have. Let us use a = 20/b.

If b = 5, a = 20/b $\rightarrow$ a = 4

If b = 8, a = 20/b $\rightarrow$ a = 2.5

So, (a, b) pairs for the sides of the original rectangle are: (4, 5) and (2.5, 8). These are found in (b) and (c) answer choices.

47. B
$\log_{10} 10,000 = x$ ... We know that $\log_a a^b = b \cdot \log_a a = b \cdot 1 = b$

$\log_{10} 10,000 = \log_{10} 10^x$ Now, we can remove $\log_{1/2}$ terms since both sides have this function applied:

$10,000 = 10^x$

$10^4 = 10^x$ If bases are the same, powers are the same:

$4 = x$

$x = 4$

48. D

The distance between two points is found by $= [(x_2 - x_1)^2 + (y_2 - y_1)^2]^{1/2}$

In this question:

$(18, 12) : x_1 = 18, y_1 = 12$

$(9, -6) : x_2 = 9, y_2 = -6$

Distance $= [(9 - 18)^2 + (-6 - 12)^2]^{1/2}$

$= [(-9)^2 + (-18)^2]^{1/2}$

$= (9^2 + 2^2 \cdot 9^2)^{1/2}$

$= (9^2(1 + 5))^{1/2}$ ... We can take 9 out of the square root:

$= 9 \cdot 6^{1/2}$

$= 9\sqrt{6}$

$= 9 \cdot 2.45$

$= 22.04$

The distance is approximately 22 units.

49. D

To understand this question better, let us draw a right triangle by writing the given data on it:

The side opposite angle a is named by a.

$\sin a$ = length of the opposite side / length of the hypotenuse = 12/13 is given.

$\cos a$ = length of the adjacent side / length of the hypotenuse = b/13

We use the Pythagorean Theorem to find the value of b:

$(Hypotenuse)^2 = (Opposite\ Side)^2 + (Adjacent\ Side)^2$

$c^2 = a^2 + b^2$

$13^2 = 12^2 + b^2$

$169 = 144 + b^2$

$b^2 = 169 - 144$

$b^2 = 25$

$b = 5$

So;
$\cos a = b/13 = 5/13$

50. D
$1/(4x - 2) = 5/6$ ... We can do cross multiplication:

$5(4x - 2) = 1\bullet6$ ... Now, we distribute 5 to the parenthesis:

$20x - 10 = 6$ ... We need x term alone on one side:

$20x = 6 + 10$

$20x = 16$ ... Dividing both sides by 20:

$x = 16/20$ ... Simplifying by 2 and having 10 in the denominator provides us finding the decimal equivalent of x:

$x = 8/10 = 0.8$

51. B
If we know the coordinates of two points on a line, we can find the slope (m) with the below formula:
$m = (y_2 - y_1)/(x_2 - x_1)$ where (x_1, y_1) represent the coordinates of one point and (x_2, y_2) the other.

In this question:

$(-4, -4) : x_1 = -4, y_1 = -4$

$(-1, 2) : x_2 = -1, y_2 = 2$

Inserting these values into the formula:

$m = (2 - (-4))/(-1 - (-4)) = (2 + 4)/(-1 + 4) = 6/3$ ... Simplifying by 3:

$m = 2$

52. A
The formula of the volume of cylinder is the base area multiplied by the height. As the formula:

Volume of a cylinder = $\pi r^2 h$. Where π is 3.142, r is radius of the cross sectional area, and h is the height.

We know that the diameter is 5 meters, so the radius is 5/2 = 2.5 meters.

The volume is: V = $3.142 \cdot 2.5^2 \cdot 12$ = 235.65 m³.

53. C
We are given that,

$a_2 = 3$

$a_{n+1} = -a_{n-1}$

Let us insert n = 2:

$a_3 = -a_4$ ... If we carry a_4 to left side:

$a_3 + a_4 = 0$ ... We were asked to find this. Without using a_2 = 3, which would not be useful in this question; we reached

this result.

54. C
The large cube is made up of 8 smaller cubes with 5 cm sides. The volume of a cube is found by the third power of the length of one side.

Volume of the large cube = Volume of the small cube$\cdot$8

= $(5^3) \cdot 8 = 125 \cdot 8$

= 1000 cm³

There is another solution for this question. Find the side length of the large cube. There are two cubes rows with 5 cm length for each. So, one side of the large cube is 10 cm.

The volume of this large cube is equal to 10^3 = 1000 cm³

55. A
First write the two equations one under the other. Our aim is to multiply equations with appropriate factors to eliminate one unknown and find the other, and then find the eliminated one using the found value.

-√5/ x√5 - y = √5 ... If we multiply this equation by √5, y terms will cancel each other:

<u>x - y√5 = 5</u>

-x√5√5 + y√5 = -√5√5 ... using √5√5 = 5:

<u>x - y√5 = 5</u>

-5x + y√5 = -5

<u>x - y√5 = 5</u> ... Summing side-by-side:

-5x + y√5 + x - y√5 = -5 + 5 ... + y√5 and - y√5, -5 and + 5 cancel each other:

-4x = 0

x = 0

Now, using either of the equations gives us the value of y. Let us choose equation 1:

x√5 - y = √5

0√5 - y = √5

-y = √5

y = -√5

The solution to the system is (0, -√5)

56. D

As shown in the figure, two parallel lines intersecting with a third line with angle of 75°.

x = 75° (corresponding angles)

x + y = 180° (supplementary angles) ... inserting the value of x here:

y = 180° - 75°
y = 105°

57. B

To understand this question better, let us draw a right triangle by writing the given data on it:

The side opposite to angle α is named by a.
The side opposite to angle β is named by b.
The hypotenuse which is the opposite side to 90° angle is named by c.

We are asked to find (sinα + cosβ)/(tgα + ctgβ).

As general formulas:

sinx = length of the opposite side / length of the hypotenuse

cosx = length of the adjacent side / length of the hypotenuse

tgx = length of the opposite side / length of the adjacent side

ctgx = length of the adjacent side / length of the opposite side

So, in this question;

sinα = a/c, cosβ = a/c, tgα = a/b, ctgβ = a/b

Inserting all known values:

(sinα + cosβ)/(tgα + ctgβ) = (a/c + a/c)/(a/b + a/b) = (2a/c)/(2a/b) = (2a/c)(b/2a) Simplifying by 2a:

= b/c

58. D
Two parallel lines (m & side AB) intersected by side AC. This means that 50° and a angles are interior angles. So:
a = 50° (interior angles).

59. D
We have a circle given with diameter 8 cm and a square located within the circle. We are asked to find the area of the circle for which we only need to know the length of the radius that is the half of the diameter.
Area of circle = πr^2 ... r = 8/2 = 4 cm

Area of circle = $\pi \cdot 4^2$

= 16π cm² ... As we notice, the inner square has no role in this question.

60. C
We see that two legs of a right triangle form by Peter's movements and we are asked to find the length of the hypotenuse. We use the Pythagorean Theorem:

(Hypotenuse)² = (Perpendicular)² + (Base)²

$h^2 = a^2 + b^2$

Given: $3^2 + 4^2 = h^2$

$h^2 = 9 + 16$

$h = \sqrt{25}$

$h = 5$

Sentence Skills

1. D
"Who" is correct because the question uses an active construction. "To whom was first place given?" is passive construction.

2. D
"Which" is correct, because the files are objects and not people.

3. C
The simple present tense, "rises," is correct.

4. A
"Lie" does not require a direct object, while "lay" does. The old woman might lie on the couch, which has no direct object, or she might lay the book down, which has the direct object, "the book."

5. D
The simple present tense, "falls," is correct because it is repeated action.

6. A
The present progressive, "building models," is correct in this sentence; it is required to match the other present progressive verbs.

7. C
Past Perfect tense describes a completed action in the past, before another action in the past.

8. D
The preposition "to" is the correct preposition to use with "bring."

9. D
"Laid" is the past tense.

10. A
This is a past unreal conditional sentence. It requires an 'if' clause and a result clause, and either clause can appear first. The 'if' clause uses the past perfect, while the result clause uses the past participle.

11. C
"But replaces "though" and must be followed by the subject "they."

12. C
"Unlike" modifies and must be closest to "green tea," which is the subject of the sentence.

13. A
"Even though" has already replaced "but"; "shark teeth, the antecedent of "they," must then begin the main clause.

14. A
"Without" substitutes for "missing."

15. A
The order is: appetizer, and then main course. "Before..." is an adverbial phrase that must modify (be close to) "Antoine ate."

16. D
The "spotting" must happen "as" Katie skates.

17. B
"Eating" must modify "bears," which must initiate a main

clause.

18. B
The comparison opened by "more rarely" must close with a "than" phrase.

19. C
"Because" offers the reason for Jeremy's condition and does so grammatically.

20. A
"Nonetheless" replaces "but," and "wishing" must modify (be closest to) "Claire."

Conclusion

CONGRATULATIONS! You have made it this far because you have applied yourself diligently to practicing for the exam and no doubt improved your potential score considerably! Getting into a good school is a huge step in a journey that might be challenging at times but will be many times more rewarding and fulfilling. That is why being prepared is so important.

Good Luck!

FREE Ebook Version

Go to
http://tinyurl.com/odp7zbu

Register for Free Updates and More Practice Test Questions

Register your purchase at
www.test-preparation.ca/register.html for fast and convenient access to updates, errata, free test tips and more practice test questions.

ACCUPLACER Test Strategy!

Learn to increase your score using time-tested secrets for answering multiple choice questions!

This practice book has everything you need to know about answering multiple choice questions on a standardized test!

You will learn 12 strategies for answering multiple choice questions and then practice each strategy with over 45 reading comprehension multiple choice questions, with extensive commentary from exam experts!

Maybe you have read this kind of thing before, and maybe feel you don't need it, and you are not sure if you are going to buy this Book.

Remember though, it only a few percentage points divide the PASS from the FAIL students.

Even if our multiple choice strategies increase your score by a few percentage points, isn't that worth it?

Go to https://www.createspace.com/4600491

Enter code LYFZGQB5 for 25% off!

Get Organized, Study Less and Get Higher Marks!

Here is what you will learn:

- How to Organize your Study Space

- Four different strategies for taking notes

- Reading strategies for textbooks, essays, novels and literature

- How to Concentrate - What is concentration and how do you do it!

- Using Flash Cards - Complete guide to using flash cards including the Leitner method.

and LOT more... Including time management, sleep, nutrition, motivation, brain food, procrastination, study schedules and more!

Go to https://www.createspace.com/4060298

Enter Code LYFZGQB5 for 25% off!

Endnotes

Reading Comprehension passages where noted below are used under the Creative Commons Attribution-ShareAlike 3.0 License

http://en.wikipedia.org/wiki/Wikipedia:Text_of_Creative_Commons_Attribution-ShareAlike_3.0_Unported_License

[1] Immune System. In *Wikipedia*. Retrieved November 12, 2010 from, en.wikipedia.org/wiki/Immune_system.
[2] Thunderstorm. In *Wikipedia*. Retrieved November 12, 2010 from en.wikipedia.org/wiki/Thunderstorm.
[3] Meteorology. In *Wikipedia*. Retrieved November 12, 2010 from en.wikipedia.org/wiki/Outline_of_meteorology.
[4] Cloud. In *Wikipedia*. Retrieved November 12, 2010 from http://en.wikipedia.org/wiki/Clouds.
[5] Respiratory System. In *Wikipedia*. Retrieved November 12, 2010 from en.wikipedia.org/wiki/Respiratory_system.
[6] Mythology. In *Wikipedia*. Retrieved November 12, 2010 from en.wikipedia.org/wiki/Mythology.
[7] Circulatory System. In *Wikipedia*. Retrieved November 12, 2010 from en.wikipedia.org/wiki/Circulatory_system